Forever
BLUENOSE

Forever BLUENOSE

A FUTURE FOR A SCHOONER WITH A PAST

Ron Crocker

Restoration photographs by Mark Doucette

NIMBUS
PUBLISHING

NIMBUS.CA

Nimbus Publishing Limited
3731 Mackintosh St, Halifax, NS B3K 5A5
(902) 455-4286 nimbus.ca

Printed and bound in China
NB1086
Design: John van der Woude Designs, www.jvdwdesigns.com
Author Photo: Mark Doucette Photographic

Library and Archives Canada Cataloguing in Publication

    Crocker, Ron
    Forever Bluenose : a future for a schooner with a past / Ron Crocker.
    Also issued in electronic format.
    ISBN 978-1-77108-056-9 (hardcover)
    ISBN 978-1-77108-128-3 (paperback)

1. Bluenose II (Ship)—History. 2. Bluenose (Ship)—History. I. Title.
VM396.B5C75 2013   387.2'2   C2013-900196-4

Nimbus Publishing acknowledges the financial support for its publishing activities from the Government of Canada through the Canada Book Fund (CBF) and the Canada Council for the Arts, and from the Province of Nova Scotia through the Department of Communities, Culture and Heritage.

For Robin Charles Fitzpatrick Crocker,
and to the memory of Charles J. Crocker

We do not simply exist in a contemporary world, our eyes fixed to the TV or computer screen, our senses bombarded by transient images and sounds. We have a past, if only we would try to grapple with it…. History matters, and we forget this truth at our peril.

—*J. L. Granatstein,* Who Killed Canadian History

CONTENTS

AUTHOR'S NOTE

All opinions and conclusions in the book are my own unless they are specifically attributed to others or contained in quotes from others who are clearly identified.

Also mine was the decision to refer to the *Bluenose* schooners and other vessels in the traditional feminine gender. Nimbus Publishing normally does not ascribe gender to inanimate objects, but agreed to this exception because of the book's subject matter and the firmly rooted nautical convention. This convention may fall eventually of its own weight, or in deference to the sensitivities of those who oppose it. While I am generally agnostic about the matter, my conviction in this case is that a book about schooners, sailing, and maritime traditions may not be the best place to break with tradition.

One other convention honoured in the book is the expression of all schooner construction measures in imperial rather than metric terms.

ACKNOWLEDGEMENTS

I owe thanks to many individuals and organizations for their help with this book.

The Lunenburg Shipyard Alliance (LSA) supported the project in important ways. LSA leaders and employees provided access to the schooner on several occasions, and patiently explained the construction process and details.

Company officials had signed non-disclosure and confidentiality agreements with the provincial government, and were understandably cautious about the business and political aspects of the project. While they were as generous as possible within the confines of those agreements, my information about the business side of the restoration project came mainly from public sources, including the province itself, and from a few sources who spoke in confidence. The schooner's design consultants, Lengkeek Vessel Engineering, Inc., politely refused to be interviewed.

Folks at the Lunenburg Foundry—Craig Buffett, Emma Kinley, and Vicki Gaulton—maintained a fat binder of notes, newspaper clippings, and photos throughout the restoration of *Bluenose II*. Vicki Gaulton allowed me to take it home for a month. The binder provided many shortcuts, especially to the local newspaper coverage.

Most important, the LSA had the foresight to hire Mark Doucette to document the entire construction project in photographs. Mark's photos really are a key justification for and an essential component of the book. Mark generously helped select and edited all of the restoration pictures.

Nimbus Publishing was helpful throughout and gave me great freedom to write. Editor Whitney Moran provided appropriate questioning and deft editorial input. Her suggestions improved the text in countless ways.

The idea to write the book was not my own. It was suggested by Sheila Fitzpatrick, my partner. Sheila also was the first of several people to read early drafts of the manuscript and provide feedback. The others were Robbie Crocker, Anne Budgell, Glenn Deir, Susan Newhook, Al Hutchison, Peter Kinley, Wade Croft, and Eric Facey. From his retirement seat in Twillingate, Newfoundland, Eric Facey, a lifelong friend and sailing mate, Skyped with me for at least ten hours, discussing the finer points of keelsons and knightheads, and declaring war on hyphens.

Ralph Getson, curator of education for the Fisheries Museum of the Atlantic in Lunenburg, was endlessly accommodating and informative. Ralph has the delightful talent of speaking in colourful, compact quotes. "Was Angus Walters a teetotaler?" I asked Ralph. "No, Blessed Father, no!"

I am grateful as well to Dan Conlin and Lynn Marie Richard of the Maritime Museum of the Atlantic for their guidance with the museum's collection of photographs, and to the Nova Scotia Archives for their user-friendly online photo display, and to the staff at the Boston Public Library for their generosity with photos from their wonderful Leslie Jones Collection.

Thanks very much to all who have helped.

Ron Crocker
Glen Haven, NS
April 2013

SCHOONER CULTURE

Spring 2011. The bones of the new *Bluenose*, like the skeleton of a majestic dinosaur, had been assembled at last in Lunenburg, Nova Scotia. John Steele, president of Covey Island Boatworks, was interviewed for a television documentary about the project. Steele looked into the camera and asked a provocative question: "How could we be without *Bluenose*? What would it say about us if we couldn't maintain *Bluenose*? If we couldn't keep a *Bluenose* sailing?"

If we lived by bread alone the answer to the question would be simple. The restoration of *Bluenose II* will cost Canadians more than $16 million, with Nova Scotians paying the lion's share. Without *Bluenose* Canadians at least would be that much richer. But there are other answers, less rooted in the public purse than in the public psyche.

If the cliché is true that *Bluenose* is more than a schooner, it is equally true that a schooner is more than a boat. Writer Harry Bruce, a lover of schooners and of the sea, saw and admired schooners through a traditional male prism:

Schooners have a strange air of dignity, power and lyricism, and it's all their own. Somewhere, you may have met a woman who was so beautiful and poised you could scarcely open your mouth. A schooner under full sail is more like her than other boats are.

Without *Bluenose*, the story of Nova Scotia's banking schooners remains an interesting history. With *Bluenose*, it is indeed more like a poem, or perhaps a romantic novel.

Lunenburg, the stolid and mysterious town that has become Bethlehem for the great schooner, also would be different without *Bluenose*. The town would continue to be a United Nations World Heritage Site. It would remain, arguably, the province's most intriguing community. Lunenburg with *Bluenose* is doubly blessed: for every visitor who arrives to see the defining British Colonial architecture and the famous Lunenburg bump, perhaps a thousand show up to admire the schooner.

Without *Bluenose*, Nova Scotia certainly would continue to be a small Maritime province with friendly people, grand scenery, and a struggling economy. *Bluenose* won't fix the economy. But with *Bluenose* Nova Scotia retains a dash of its nineteenth-century spirit of independence, in both trading and politics. *Bluenose* helps connect Nova Scotians to past glories, helps keep a twinkle in their eyes and a spring in their steps.

The original 1920 schooner, her designer William Roué, and her mercurial skipper Angus Walters all inspired Canadian postage stamps. *Bluenose*, as every Canadian child knows, is on our dime. And as bluesman Morgan Davis regularly reminds us, "we got the *Bluenose* on our license plates."

Preservation of *Bluenose* and protection of schooner culture are taken for granted by the vast majority of Nova Scotians, by legions of other Canadians, and by political players of all stripes. The matter of the schooner's continued existence appears to be non-negotiable, a Canadian truth held to be self-evident.

And that's the way it is.

By late winter 2011, the new Bluenose *hull had taken shape inside the work shed. She would be the most durable version of* Bluenose *ever built.*

Chapter I

LONG LIVE THE QUEEN

I march across great waters like a queen,

I whom so many wisdoms helped to make.

-John Masefield

And if I had me sooners, I'd sooner have a schooner…

-Buddy Wasisname and the Other Fellers

The love affair has lasted nearly a century. *Bluenose*, the great racing schooner. *Bluenose II*, the replica. *Bluenose II* restored. Schooner *Bluenose* of the famous MacAskill photographs. *Bluenose* on dimes, stamps, and license plates. *Bluenose* forever; apparently forever young.

Bluenose inspires wry affection everywhere. A trendy Haligonian refers to her affectionately as "the Schnoz." A cluster of adolescent guitar players named a band for her, "The Bluenose Pickers." Bluenose tattoos are not uncommon. And she has inspired some of the most ornate prose ever written. A typical example, evoking the age of the newsreel, appeared in the *Halifax Chronicle-Herald* on January 31, 1946—the day after *Bluenose* sank off Haiti.

> *Nova Scotia's far-famed champion, the fleet-limbed and stout-hearted racing schooner Bluenose which outran every sailing vessel on the*

OPPOSITE

The original Bluenose *sails smartly into Halifax harbour in 1931, "fleet-limbed and stout-hearted" in the words of one writer. A year earlier, in "mid-career,"* Bluenose *had lost a race to the* Gertrude L. Thebaud *when the Fishermen's Cup was not at stake, but defeated her handily in 1931 when it was.*

Atlantic but couldn't escape her destiny, has found a harbour deep beneath West Indies waters....

Stripped of her billowing expanse of white canvas which made her undisputed mistress of wind-driven craft, the Bluenose took the final plunge alone. None of the crew of eight went down with her.

But we must mock with great caution. It would be unwise for any *Bluenose* chronicler to feign indifference to the charms of the great schooner, and to pretend they do not strive to elevate their own prose to the levels of her achievements.

The long saga of *Bluenose* has a clear beginning, but no obvious middle, and now, with a new and improved *Bluenose* in the water, no imminent end. It all started on March 6, 1921, when the original *Bluenose* was launched in Lunenburg. She cost $35,580 to build, money raised by selling 350 shares at $100 each, most of which were bought by Lunenburg and Halifax businessmen. Angus Walters of Lunenburg bought ninety shares himself, and was named both captain and managing director.

Another major milestone in the great saga occurred on July 24, 1963. On that day *Bluenose II*, a near-perfect replica of her famous forebear, was launched in Lunenburg to lusty cheers and general delight. Hats were tossed high in the air. Older Lunenburgers had longed for that day since the original *Bluenose* was lost in 1946. An unlikely turn of events in the early 1960s had renewed their hopes, and put Lunenburg back in the wooden-schooner business.

By 1960 more than half a century had passed since Nova Scotia's world-renowned shipbuilders had deployed their adzes and caulking irons on a project of such magnitude. In a curious way, the person who changed all of that, and much else, was Fletcher Christian, the mutineer. The actual mutiny on the *Bounty* took place in 1789. But 1960 was the year Lunenburg's Smith & Rhuland Shipyard was asked to build a replica of Her Majesty's Ship *Bounty* by the motion picture giant Metro-Goldwyn-Mayer. MGM was about to produce what would become one of the most famous movies of the twentieth century, *Mutiny on the Bounty*, starring Marlon Brando.

Hollywood knows filmmaking; Lunenburg knows wooden boats. Out came the whetstones, the spokeshaves, and the six-foot augers. Out came the myriad latent skills of wooden-boat construction like rare plants too long in shadow, ready to bloom the day the sun saw fit to shine. Construction of *Bounty* in 1960 became an unlikely but important component of the *Bluenose* story. It demonstrated that the skills necessary to replicate a wooden vessel from the 1780s remained intact in Lunenburg County, as if preserved in the local DNA. And if *Bounty* could be rebuilt, why not *Bluenose*?

Lunenburg was appropriately proud of *Bounty*. And on the morning of October 29, 2012, when the sad news broke, many Lunenburgers grieved. Nearing her fiftieth year of making movies, training sailors, and general admiration, *Bounty* had become a casualty of Superstorm Sandy and had sunk off the coast of North Carolina. Her skipper for twenty years, sixty-three-year-old Robin Walbridge, and crewmember Claudene Christian, died in the water. Christian, who was forty-three, had been attracted to *Bounty* in part because the mutineer Fletcher Christian was a family ancestor, many "greats" ago.

Marjorie Zwicker of Auburndale, Lunenburg County, wept that October day. Her husband, Gerald Zwicker, had helped build the ship in 1960, subsequently working on *Bluenose II*. In the summer of 2012, when *Bounty* was in Halifax for a Tall Ships showcase, Claudene Christian had promoted a visit by *Bounty* to Lunenburg, where crewmembers had met some of the aging *Bounty* shipwrights, including Gerald.

Such are the connections between Lunenburg and its boats; between the people who build them and the people who sail them. Such are the connections between the people of Nova Scotia and their flagship schooner, *Bluenose*.

TWO ENDS AND A BEGINNING

By 2009, *Bluenose II*, nearly half a century old—two lifetimes in traditional schooner years—was hogged. A schooner is hogged when age and infirmity cause her bow and stern to slump downward, warping her entire structure and gradually flattening the natural upward arc between stem and stern. Wooden vessels, especially those made of the softer woods of Atlantic Canada, absorb vast

The "restored" Bluenose II, a.k.a Bluenose Now, about to be launched into Lunenburg Harbour on the drizzly morning of September 29, 2012. The hull is completely new, but much of the deck furnishings, interior hardwoods, and standing and running rigging were salvaged from the dismantled old Bluenose II.

quantities of water. So soaked and heavy had the original *Bluenose* become by 1938 (the year she won her final race) that she required 40 percent less ballast than when she was first launched in 1921.

Both fore and aft, long sections of a schooner, called overhangs, remain out of the water. Gravity pushes those sections downward as the water floats the midsection upward. The profile of the vessel gradually changes to look more like a hog than a schooner. Wilson Fitt, the builders' project manager for the *Bluenose II* restoration, has a more prosaic explanation: "A schooner is like a person. When she gets old, her arse falls."

Something had to be done. Nova Scotia has always held *Bluenose* as a symbol of enterprise and self-sufficiency, and as a monument to the heroic and tragic banking schooner past. Nova Scotia without *Bluenose* was unthinkable. In the *Bluenose* tradition an idea was born, or, more accurately, reborn. Why not build a new *Bluenose*?

No, said the bureaucrats. There is no money to build a new *Bluenose*. It was, after all, 2009, already many months into the most dramatic recession since the first *Bluenose* was a teenager. Then why not restore *Bluenose II*? Yes, said the bureaucrats. The economy must be stimulated to forestall further decline. There is money for the restoration of important historic monuments and for economic infrastructure. *Bluenose II* is infrastructure? She is now.

On a damp September 29, 2012, the "restored" hull of *Bluenose II*—for convenience let's call her "Bluenose Now"—was inched safely and slowly into the welcoming waters of Lunenburg harbour. As the water rose over the massive rolling platform that carried her across the landwash, she floated comfortably; light but fair on her lines, her high and haughty bow already displaying attitude.

Built into the fo'c'sle and the officers' cabins of Bluenose Now are the same mahogany bunk boards that kept sailors in their bunks when the old schooner rolled down in a breeze. Crew quarters and officers' cabin furnishings have been restored and reinstalled. Windlasses from *Bluenose II* have been repaired for reuse.

By late October 2012, the towering Douglas fir masts that *Bluenose II* had carried for years had been stepped through the Douglas fir decks of the brand new hull. They are secured aloft by the same standing rigging used on *Bluenose II*.

In the spring of 2013, the sails of the *Bluenose II*, mended and maintained, would be bent back on. Scattered throughout Bluenose Now are many other salvaged wood and metal items from the old schooner, chips off the old block. They include deck furnishings and companion ways made of Honduras mahogany, twenty tons of lead ballast, and numerous metal components such as hawse pipes, fairleads, chocks and belaying pins. This rescue of Bluenose II components was carefully done. It is this material that represents the "restoration" aspect of the schooner, the hull of which is completely new.

In 2009, when the federal and Nova Scotia governments first got behind the *Bluenose* renewal concept, there was little debate about whether schooner *Bluenose* would survive. There was considerable debate over whether "survival" would mean a new schooner or a restored schooner, and what exactly a restored schooner might be.

Many Lunenburg shipbuilding experts and countless wharf senators shared a clear position on this matter: build a new schooner and call her *Bluenose III*. She would cost less and potentially be a more cohesive and durable piece of work. Nova Scotia politicians thought differently. Significant federal money could be available for a restoration, which also included waterfront commercial facilities such as the new side-transfer system. This facility allows a vessel to be built on three rolling steel platforms that can be cranked across to a launching platform when the job is done.

The waterfront developments and a restored schooner to promote tourism tucked the project under

a recession-inspired federal funding umbrella set up to create "economic drivers," also known as jobs. The program might cover half the cost of getting *Bluenose* back on the ocean. Provincial tourism officials wished to retain as much of the old *Bluenose II* as possible, for legacy reasons, and because they believed they could reduce costs by using salvaged components of the old boat. They also believed *Bluenose II* had built her own status and recognition, her own brand, which was deemed a valuable asset in itself.

There was much speculation, too, that the province wanted to avoid any suggestion that an entirely new boat was being built, raising the issue of whether the original William J. Roué design plans were being used. The Roué family and the province are at odds over

For both nostalgic and economic reasons, the Government of Nova Scotia decided to reuse as many components and materials as possible from the old Bluenose II. *The "minister-furnished equipment," as it was called, was carefully removed from the old schooner, tagged, and set aside in a Lunenburg warehouse, awaiting the new* Bluenose *hull.*

recognition of Roué's contribution to Bluenose Now, as the original *Bluenose* designer. In October of 2012, a lawsuit was launched by the Roué family, claiming the province either used Roué's materials without the family's permission—an unacceptable slight—or else it did not, in which case, the suit alleged, the province does not have an authentic *Bluenose*.

REBUILT, RESTORED, RELAUNCHED

On that drizzly September morning in Lunenburg, hundreds of well-wishers and *Bluenose* junkies got Tim-Hortoned and yellow-slickered to witness the early launch, timed for high tide at 8:10 A.M., while thousands more watched on national television or online. Many were moved by the spectacle and the symbolism of the occasion. Whenever the word "restoration" was uttered in Lunenburg on launch day, there were bemused grins all round, and good-natured nudges and winks.

If there ever was a genuine "restoration versus rebuilding" dilemma, semantics provided an instant solution. Under arcane and unofficial rules for ship replicas, the restoration bar is set rather low. Ordinary and common sense notions are honoured mainly in the breach. A schooner can be totally rebuilt but still be considered a "restoration" as long as "some" components of the original are carried forward into the new boat. Lunenburg songwriter Tom Gallant—a schooner owner himself and a keen observer of schooner affairs—allowed that only a bit of air from *Bluenose II* needed to be blown through the new boat for her to meet the threshold. But the Lunenburg Shipyard Alliance, the private company formed to rebuild the schooner, was more generous. They created a reasonable list of items to reuse: spars, mahogany from the bunks and cabinetry, standing rigging, and sails. In the builders' contracting documents, the salvaged components are designated as "minister-furnished equipment."

On launch day none of this minister-furnished homage to the deconstructed *Bluenose II* could salvage the worst-kept secret in Lunenburg. Nova Scotians and all Canadians now possess a brand new *Bluenose*, rebuilt from her keel to her cap rails. More solidly built than ever, Bluenose Now adheres as closely as possible to the genetic code of *Bluenose II*, just as *Bluenose II* honoured, but did not strictly duplicate, the original.

The Canadian Register of Vessels will recognize the new boat officially as *Bluenose II*. And she is *Bluenose II* for the purpose that matters most: getting someone to pay for her. Unofficially, of course, the world will call her the *Bluenose*.

Chapter II

UNDER FULL CANVAS: *BLUENOSE* 1921

Nova Scotians [in 1920] badly needed something to cheer about. The publisher [William Dennis] found that something in the province's seafaring tradition….
-*William March,* Red Line: The Chronicle-Herald and the Mail Star 1875–1954

When Captain Angus Walters of *Bluenose* would glance astern at his racing rivals—a pleasure he often enjoyed—he'd spy scores of Nova Scotia fishermen on the foredecks of the vessels in his wake. Not only were many of the swift American schooners behind him modelled shamelessly on *Bluenose,* they were often crewed and skippered by Walters's fellow Nova Scotians.

The 1922 Fisherman's Trophy Race was typical. The challenger to *Bluenose* that year was a new schooner, *Henry Ford,* Boston-funded and captained by Clayton

"Clayt" Morrissey, a friend of Angus who hailed from Lower East Pubnico in southwest Nova Scotia. Indeed, Morrissey's family pedigree demonstrates just how intertwined the International Fishermen's Trophy races were with the wider schooner culture of Lunenburg, Nova Scotia, and that of Gloucester, Massachusetts.

If *Bluenose* is the world's most famous fishing schooner, the *Effie M. Morrissey* is one of her closest celebrity rivals, known first as a banker out of Gloucester and then Digby, and subsequently as Newfoundland explorer Captain Bob Bartlett's beloved Arctic expedition

vessel in the 1930s and '40s. The namesake of the *Effie M. Morrissey* was Clayt Morrissey's younger sister. Their father had been her first skipper.

Nearly all of the Gloucestermen (both schooners and the men who sailed them are referred to as such) were extensively crewed by men from the Pubnicos and southwestern Nova Scotia, along with a fair smattering of Newfoundlanders, men recruited only incidentally for their schooner-racing skills, but primarily for their toughness and fishing prowess. The Nova Scotia skippers, like Morrissey and Marty Welch, represented Gloucester in much the same way Sidney Crosby represents Pittsburgh today.

The famous schooner races of the 1920s were for the International Fishermen's Trophy, but in many ways they were all about Nova Scotia honour and pride. The races were, of course, a Nova Scotia creation. In 1921 William H. Dennis, then editor and publisher of the *Halifax Herald* and the *Evening Mail*, issued a "Deed of Gift" for the schooner races. It was a document of high formality, written in the arch and formal language of the age.

> *To all Men Greetings…be it known that William H. Dennis…recognizing the great importance and value of the deep sea fishing industry to the inhabitants of this Province of Nova Scotia, Canada….*

And on it went, through a dense preamble and fourteen detailed clauses, to announce "The Halifax Herald and Evening Mail Nova Scotia Fishing Vessel Championship Trophy…as a perpetual International Trophy, to be raced for annually." The deed not only provided the trophy, it covered a hundred other details, from ballast allocations to sail yardage to the maximum waterline length of the schooners. If there was ambiguity in some of the deed's clauses, there was clarity in at least two: the only vessels permitted to compete would be "bona-fide fishing vessels which have been engaged in commercial deep sea fishing for at least one season." And only "bona-fide fishermen" could comprise the crews and captains.

Bluenose competed for the Fishermen's Trophy five times, first in 1921 and finally in 1938. She won four of those races cleanly, retaining the trophy and enjoying the prize money. In the disputed 1923 race against *Columbia*, her finest US rival, *Bluenose* clearly outsailed *Columbia* in two races. But the second race was awarded to the Gloucester schooner on a technicality, Angus Walters having passed a buoy on the wrong side. As the series was best two out of three, Angus declared victory anyway and sailed *Bluenose* back to Lunenburg from Halifax. Officially, the race was incomplete. The schooners split the prize money, but the trophy stayed in Lunenburg.

OPPOSITE
Over two decades, the original Bluenose *under Captain Angus Walters faced challenges from several worthy Gloucester and Boston schooners—often skippered by Nova Scotians. Here,* Bluenose, *left, sail #1, does combat with Gloucester's* Henry Ford, *commanded by Captain Clayton Morrissey of Pubnico, Nova Scotia.* Bluenose *won; her second of five Fishermen's Trophy victories.*

After outsailing her finest rival, Ben Pine's Columbia (left), in two races in 1923, Angus Walters claimed victory for Bluenose and went home. However, the second race was awarded to Columbia *on a technicality and officially the series was deemed inconclusive, causing a ruckus and contributing to a seven-year hiatus in international racing. The two well-matched schooners would never meet again.* Columbia *was lost in a 1927 storm, killing all of her twenty-three Nova Scotian crewmembers.*

The involvement of so many Nova Scotians on the American side gave the races a uniquely local intensity. Adding to the thrill was the fact that to qualify as the Canadian contender, *Bluenose* usually had to fend off several Nova Scotia challengers in run-off races that engendered almost as much excitement as the cross-border finals. The success of *Bluenose* was not universally applauded in Nova Scotia, and she had powerful competitors at home. Often those rivals reflected the pride of other shipbuilding centres, such as LaHave or Shelburne, spiked by a degree of resentment of almighty Lunenburg, the Maritimes' most prosperous fishing town. William Roué himself, proud as he was of

Bluenose, was a player in one such initiative to create a worthy homegrown rival. Roué may have had his own motivation; he claimed he was never fully compensated for his *Bluenose* design.

Haligonian, the William Roué-designed Nova Scotia challenger, was put forward in 1925, purpose-built in Shelburne, and, as her name implies, backed by Halifax money. The theory was that if Roué could design the successful *Bluenose*, who but he could design her better? In the much-anticipated October 1926 showdown, the crew of the *Haligonian* saw a lot of *Bluenose*'s stern. Four races were held and two counted officially. All were won handily by *Bluenose*. *Haligonian*'s skipper, Moyle Crouse, was interviewed after the final race. "We did the best we could," he said, "but *Haligonian*'s best wasn't good enough today. Excuse me. I want to go over and congratulate Angus."

YES, BUT...

When schooner aficionados discuss their favourite subject, assessments of *Bluenose*'s sailing merits, of her successes and failures, usually are met with a "Yes, but."

Yes, but, it was said, *Haligonian* had gone ashore in the Strait of Canso the previous summer and had been damaged and warped.

Yes, but *Bluenose* had also gone ashore the previous summer in Placentia Bay, Newfoundland, under the command of Angus's brother, Captain John "Sonny" Walters.

Yes, but when *Haligonian* subsequently did outsail *Bluenose*—in an informal "hook" returning from the Banks, and at a Lunenburg fishermen's picnic—*Bluenose* was said to be showing her age and wear.

Schooner *Mahaska*, out of Shelburne, was another local schooner built to beat *Bluenose*. Her spiritual owners put their faith in superstition, not by honouring Chief Mahaska of the Iowan tribe, but by honouring the vowels in his name. A nautical superstition holds that a vessel is charmed if her name contains three vowels, preferably A's. Local *Bluenose* rivals such as *Delawana* and *Canadia* pursued similar strategies, with similar results. Andrew Merkel, author of the 1948 book *Schooner Bluenose*, observes that the *Mahaska* owners "were not concerned so much with the centre of effort, a key element in a vessel's stability, as with the spelling of the schooner's name. This in order to bestow the requisite amount of luck was required to include one of the vowels, at least thrice repeated."

It generally was believed, Merkel reported, that *Mahaska* was faster than *Bluenose* on all points of sail: "But *Bluenose*'s weatherly qualities proceeded from something more substantial than the spelling of her name, and *Mahaska* was beaten by twenty minutes in a thirty mile race. Whereat, Captain Paddy Mack, her skipper, threw his hard hat on the deck and jumped the stuffing out of it."

SCHOONER WITH A MISSION

The Nova Scotia obsession with the International Fishermen's Trophy races did nothing to diminish their appeal to both Americans and Canadians. They became cross-border sensations.

Bluenose, the Lunenburg warrior that ultimately trounced all comers, held a special niche in the hearts of all Nova Scotians who paid attention. *Bluenose* not only outran the best schooners the well-heeled Americans could throw at her for two decades, but Angus and

his *Bluenose* crew could out-savvy and outsail the best schooner skippers and crews in the world, their fellow Nova Scotians foremost among them.

One feature of *Bluenose* mythology is that the original was a fishing schooner first and a racing schooner only incidentally. Another is that she represented the heyday of banking schooner fishing. Neither is correct. *Bluenose* indeed was an outstanding fishing schooner, and her skipper, Angus Walters, was an established highliner. But *Bluenose* was built to race and Angus was built to race her. He was, in the words of a contemporary, "a bugger to carry sail."

Bluenose arrived in the twilight of the banking schooner era. The golden age peaked in the late 1880s, when, according to historian Mike Parker, Lunenburg County had 193 salt bankers and 4,842 fishermen, and Nova Scotia contributed more than a third of the value of the entire Canadian fishery. By 1920 the idea of building a great banking schooner was more about honouring the past than fishing in the present.

The Fishermen's Cup schooner races were international, but fierce run-off competitions often preceded them, as local schooners and skippers sought the coveted right to represent Nova Scotia, and Canada incidentally. In 1926, Halifax investors entered the Haligonian, *constructed in Shelburne and designed, as was* Bluenose *(left), by William J. Roué.* Bluenose *won.*

In *Red Line*, his history of the *Halifax Chronicle-Herald* and the *Mail Star* to 1954, William March captures the social and economic dynamic of the day. In March's account, there was more going on with the schooner races than the mere spectacle of handsome vessels in full dress, driven by the world's greatest sailors. "One of the wants, if not the needs, of the masses, as Dennis correctly suspected, was excitement," March writes. "Nova Scotians, he felt, had the same taste for the sensational as had human beings elsewhere, but preferred it in discreet dress."

In 1920 there occurred an event in the world of international yacht racing that left *Herald* editor W. H. Dennis roary-eyed. As Keith McLaren describes the situation in *A Race for Real Sailors*, the America's Cup, the competition for gilt-edged yachts built exclusively to race, had become the world's premier yachting event.

On July 24, 1920, two slender-hulled sailboats jockeyed around in the turbulent waters off Sandy Hook, New York, awaiting a decision from the committee boat nearby. Both the British Shamrock IV *and the American* Resolute *were rigged for weather, their mains reefed and their storm sails forward. The masters of these two thoroughbreds watched for the sign that the race was on.*

Incredibly, the race was not to be. With a heavy sea running, the committee boat proposed calling it off. Both skippers complied, each man fearing potential vessel damage that could cost him the race. One reporter wrote that it blew "only a wholesale breeze," peaking at twenty-eight miles per hour, no more than "half a gale." The crowd on hand was disappointed and a little skeptical. But in the world of "real sailors," headquartered largely in Lunenburg, Nova Scotia, and in Gloucester, Massachusetts, there was universal cynicism, with gusts to pure contempt.

"The series was discussed, chewed over, and spat out in disgust by fishermen from Massachusetts to Newfoundland," McLaren recounts. "The timidity of the America's Cup yachtsmen was too much for the fishermen of the North Atlantic, and they began to talk about a real test, a contest between the men who worked the schooners that sailed the great offshore banks. Now that would be a race."

William Dennis knew the newspaper business. He also knew his province and his times. In the 1920s and '30s his papers demonstrated considerable empathy for working-class Nova Scotians in tough times, showing so much support for striking coal miners in Cape Breton that one rival paper, marching to yet another Great Depression drum, noted the *Herald*'s "Bolshevistic" tendencies. W. H. Dennis, a lifelong Tory supporter and a future Canadian senator, was hardly a communist, but there were few Cape Breton union bosses more attuned than he to the modulating moods of the masses.

Other economic and political currents were at play as well, and all invited the kind of response the schooner races provided. Nova Scotia's century-old schooner and dory fishery was in serious decline. New-fashioned gas and diesel engines were enabling trawlers to out-fish the schooners with far fewer men. The traditional north-south trade that had made Nova Scotia comparatively prosperous in the past was fading. East–west rail traffic gradually shifted the Maritimes' economic dynamic from selling and trading goods with buyers south of the border to importing goods from Ontario and Quebec.

In a bleak foreshadowing of our own times, appeals to limit Atlantic trawler activity in the interest of both fish stocks and jobs were heard politely in Ottawa, and promptly ignored. The "Maritime Rights" political banner was widely saluted, and the Dennis newspapers were totally on board. It is worth remembering that 1920 was only fifty-three years after the 1867 British North America Act. And it is also worth noting that in the 1860s, when Joseph Howe led the Nova Scotia resistance to the "Botheration Scheme" of Confederation, one of his rallying cries was that control of the fisheries was being "bargained away." If you listen closely today, a chorus of Amens might still be heard in Lunenburg, echoed throughout Nova Scotia and Newfoundland as well.

Against this brittle mix of Nova Scotia patriotism, Maritime chauvinism, and widespread deprivation, the idea of a great international schooner race was perfect. It would honour and help protect the indigenous trades, and, not incidentally, it would show the effete yachtsmen of Boston, and the "canoe-minded" crowd in Ottawa, as the *Herald* once called them, how things ought to be done.

Chapter III
THE SCHOONER THAT BEER BUILT

The only noble thing a man can do with money is build a schooner.

-Robert Louis Stevenson

When Publisher William Dennis promoted the *Bluenose* project in 1920 and, through his newspapers, assailed and mocked the Ottawa minions who discouraged it, he did so not just under the widely saluted "Maritime Rights" banner. He also did so with the competitive spirit of a successful businessman: one hand on his heart and the other on his wallet. Schooner racing and culture were not just good for the Nova Scotian soul, they were bonanzas for the circulation of Dennis's papers.

In 1963, when Colonel Sidney Oland decided to spend $208,000 of the Oland family fortune to build *Bluenose II*, his own weather eye was as much on the sales of Schooner lager as on the sails of schooner *Bluenose*. For a decade thereafter, *Bluenose II* did what was asked of her, essentially working as a private yacht promoting the Schooner brand. By 1970 the Olands were confronting the already daunting maintenance costs of a seven-year-old wooden schooner. They also were in the process of selling their family business to Labatt Ltd. Weary of

an aging schooner and soggy money, the family tied up *Bluenose II* and stood down her crew. A year later the Olands transferred the traditional sixty-four ownership shares of the vessel to the Province of Nova Scotia for one dollar, reputedly paid with ten *Bluenose* dimes.

In his 1984 book *Schooner: Bluenose and Bluenose II*, Silver Donald Cameron captured the Olands' dilemma perfectly: "She might have fetched $750,000 on the market, rot and all. But how could they sell Nova Scotia's symbolic ship, particularly to a buyer anywhere else?" On the September day in 2012 when the restored *Bluenose II* was launched, an Oland family member was quoted as saying the family had had many offers to buy *Bluenose II* in the early 1970s, but had elected not to sell, except to the province. Most adult Nova Scotians today have either grown up or grown old with *Bluenose II*. For them, she is "the *Bluenose*," and her presence over half a century, if generally taken for granted, has preserved a connection with an increasingly opaque past.

With the Olands out and the province in, *Bluenose II* soon became a moonstruck schooner whose popularity and reputation waxed and waned. To some extent it wavered with the popularity and commitment of the successive Nova Scotia governments that owned her. Despite the best of intentions, and indeed despite many successes, *Bluenose II* did not always enjoy complete clarity of purpose. As an aging wooden schooner, she also suffered from frequent physical neglect.

BREAKERS AHEAD

By the early 1980s, *Bluenose II*, well past adolescence, appeared to be destined for a more sedate role, a more sober and courtly life. But it was not always that way.

If *Bluenose II* achieved a quieter dignity in the 1980s; the serenity followed a more flamboyant youth. Much of the schooner's later life—taking sightseers on tours of Halifax Harbour at ten dollars a head—seemed like atonement for a misspent past. Some stories of early *Bluenose II* adventures may be apocryphal, a few have turned into a kind of charming folklore, but many others are well-documented. Writer Silver Donald Cameron recorded many of the 1970s *Bluenose II* antics in detail. In 1983 Cameron sailed on *Bluenose II* as a kind of working passenger from Lunenburg to Atlantic City, getting to know the crew and listening to their yarns. The 1970s *Bluenose II* adventures are also recalled by Captain Don Barr, a *Bluenose* veteran who sailed with the schooner for most of those years, as bo'sun and then first mate.

Like a wayward ghost ship, *Bluenose II* in the early to mid-1970s wandered around US and Canadian ports in

OPPOSITE
The storied career of the original Bluenose II *was launched on July 24, 1963. The Oland family of Halifax, which built her, planned to keep her for about eight years, and in 1971 they turned her over to the province.*

frequent party mode, ramming docks, beer bottles rolling on her deck, and dark headlines greeting her sometimes unwelcome landfalls. During much of her first decade of public ownership the name "*Bluenose*" became for the first time in history a term of embarrassment and derision, leavened only by the schooner's real, if sporadic, triumphs as a tourism promoter. Cameron called the era "the Gilbert and Sullivan phase" of the schooner's life.

A 1974 tour in the US was typical. Entering Norfolk, Virginia, *Bluenose II* rammed a piling and damaged her bowsprit. But perhaps her most ignominious moment came when she visited Gloucester, Massachusetts, ancient redoubt of the leading tribe of *Bluenose* detractors and antagonists. *Bluenose II* entered the harbour "under full diesel," read the headline in the local Gloucester paper. Angus Walters, six years dead by then, may have turned in his grave.

Under a new master, Ernest Hartling, a retired Halifax Harbour pilot, *Bluenose II* set out in the spring of 1975 to visit the Great Lakes, trolling for tourists. In Montreal, heading upriver, holding tanks for a new sewerage system had to be installed temporarily on deck, and word spread in Ontario that *Bluenose II* did not have adequate sewage disposal to meet Ontario's newly torqued environmental regulations. A minor inter-provincial diplomatic incident ensued, made worse when the Nova Scotia tourism

minister of the day dismissed the negative publicity as "a total pile of crap."

The following year, en route to New Orleans, Captain Hartling ordered an unscheduled stop in Fort Lauderdale, Florida, where *Bluenose II* shipped aboard Mary Smith of Cleveland, Ohio, a woman with whom Captain Hartling had launched a May-December relationship (she was forty-three, and he seventy at the time) the previous year. As both Donald Cameron and Captain Don Barr are careful to point out, spouses and select friends frequently travelled on board *Bluenose II*. Unwed, at least to each other, Captain Hartling and Mary Smith were indeed devotees of one another who eventually married, under a halo of high romance. Unfortunately, the Mary Smith affair became a minor public scandal back in Nova Scotia with the worst possible results: it embarrassed the schooner's political masters.

There are different versions of what actually happened. Cameron's colourful account was that the captain introduced Mary at an event as the *Bluenose*'s new purser. Reporters licked their chops and the news broke in Canada in a flash. Captain Hartling subsequently told a biographer that this story was untrue, but that a version of it actually had originated with a reporter in Mobile, Alabama. Whatever the turn of events, in Philadelphia, on the return trip, Nova Scotia's deputy minister of

tourism boarded *Bluenose II* and relieved Captain Hartling of command, installing Captain Andrew Thomas in his place.

The voyage had been bad news all round. Among other calamities, *Bluenose* got stuck in the Mississippi mud, arrived too early for a planned welcoming ceremony in New Orleans, and tied up at the wrong wharf. Before the fateful stop in Philadelphia, *Bluenose II* had visited Washington, where Prime Minister Pierre Trudeau was scheduled to go aboard. This drew a crowd, and with a flock of reporters and curious onlookers standing on the dock, *Bluenose II* made an out-of-control landing, her suddenly swinging foresail boom endangering persons on the dock, and picking up a section of chain-link fence with her bowsprit. Don Barr recounts this incident today as a failure on the part of the captain to give unambiguous orders in the face of a last-minute wind shift.

Scandal notwithstanding, Ernest Hartling was one of *Bluenose II*'s more intriguing skippers. Don Barr recalls Hartling's morning ritual of a tot of rum with the chief engineer sharply at 10 A.M. And in the pages of Jo Kranz's *Bluenose Master: The Memoirs of Captain Ernest K. Hartling*, the captain casts himself as a seaman of experience and integrity—a reputation Hartling came by honestly through a half-century of seafaring. In his version of *Bluenose* events, as told to Kranz, Hartling emerges as an independent-minded mariner, buffeted and frustrated by the ineptitude of amateur crewmembers too often rewarded for partisan political loyalty, and by the general perfidy of politicians and sundry other hangashores. Jo Kranz re-tells the story of Pierre Trudeau's Washington visit to *Bluenose II* as a highlight of the beleaguered captain's command. Manning up to a potentially embarrassing situation, Captain Hartling introduced Mary Smith as his future bride. "Ah," the prime minister reportedly said, "*une affaire de coeur*." "*Oui*," Ernest agreed, grinning, "*un coup de foudre*." Love at first sight; a bolt from the blue.

By mid-summer Captain Andrew Thomas had delivered *Bluenose* safely home to Halifax, both schooner and crew somewhat the worst for wear. To her eternal credit, and a tribute to public affection for the schooner, *Bluenose II* weathered the storms of the 1970s, sailing successfully on for three more decades.

Chapter IV
KEEPING HER AFLOAT

It's like standing in the shower, ripping up hundred dollar bills....

-Boat-owner's lament

You could put [*Bluenose*] in a barn in the middle of the province and people would
still flock to see her.

-Ralph Getson

Restorations of *Bluenose II* were not invented in 2010. Over the many years of *Bluenose II*'s physical suffering, provincial governments responded slowly to her stresses. But they always responded.

Bluenose II, built for $208,000 in 1963, enjoyed her first major refit in 1973–74 at a cost of $250,000. Nova Scotia and Ottawa contributed $155,000. The Oland family contributed $50,000, a magnanimous gesture

coming four years after they had sold the schooner to the people of Nova Scotia for a dollar. A portion of the remaining cost was offset by a fundraising campaign led by Dartmouth broadcaster Arnie Patterson, who mobilized school children across Canada to send in *Bluenose* dimes.

In 1983 the Progressive Conservative government of Premier John Buchanan spent another $500,000 to refurbish *Bluenose*. Most of her oak planks and timbers

were renewed. What shipwrights call bright-work—the varnished wood and polished brass that helps transform objects into art—was largely re-burnished or replaced. Her lifeboat dories were replaced, at $1,150 apiece.

Perhaps the closest any government ever came to abandoning *Bluenose* was in 1993–94 when she was condemned and tied up at the Lunenburg Museum wharf. The PC government of that day announced that she would sail no more. Influential people advocated scuttling her. Then the government changed and John Savage's Liberals came along. One significant and positive outcome of the 1994 crisis was the establishment of the non-profit *Bluenose II* Preservation Trust under Senator Wilfred Moore. This organization had the province's blessing to take over *Bluenose* funding and operations, but with one stressful caveat: they were advised in September of 1994 that *Bluenose II* needed to be available for the prestigious G7 Summit scheduled to take place in Halifax the following June.

It was to be a command performance, commanded in fact by the prime minister of the day, Jean Chrétien. In her biography of her great-grandfather, William Roué, Joan Roué says the G7 played a huge role in the life of *Bluenose II*. In effect, it saved the schooner by corralling government funding just in time, enabling her most extensive refit ever during the winter of 1995. This time it was John Savage's Liberal government that spent the provincial money to restore *Bluenose II*, including a replacement of her decaying ninety-foot mainmast. By then, thirty years old and initially purchased by the province for those ten *Bluenose* dimes, she had cost Canadian taxpayers well over $1 million. Very few eyebrows were raised, and there was the usual evidence of public support for and pride in *Bluenose*. At around that time, a survey by the Nova Scotia Economic Renewal Agency revealed that seven out of ten Nova Scotians were on-side and in fact favoured building a new *Bluenose* over repairing the old schooner.

Phillip Snyder of Snyder's Shipyard Ltd. oversaw that refit, which his company carried out in Lunenburg, supported by Lunenburg Industrial Foundry and Engineering Ltd. According to Snyder, 60 percent of *Bluenose II*'s framing was replaced, along with 80 percent of her planking, the second such major overhaul in *Bluenose II* history. The schooner's inadequate ventilation system, deemed largely responsible for her extensive and premature structural rot, was upgraded. The refurbished vessel emerged in the spring with a Canadian Coast Guard Class One license. This certified her integrity and seaworthiness for the following four years, bringing the aging schooner to within a short beam reach of the new century.

OPPOSITE

In this photo, Bluenose II, reefed and ready, makes progress in a seaway. She had seen rougher weather. On her maiden voyage in 1963 she ran into a hurricane, with eighty-two-year-old Angus Walters on board as a kind of skipper emeritus. Angus carried his own barometer, and said afterwards that he "had never seen a glass fall as quickly" as it had in the one hundred-knot winds the new schooner encountered.

Normal wear and tear and the softer local woods of which she was built, meant constant and costly maintenance for Bluenose II. In 1973, only a decade old, she was tied up and ready for her first major refit at the Smith and Rhuland wharf in Lunenburg.

Bluenose's estimated $500,000 refit was completed in the spring of 1995 below budget at $418,000. The province contributed $90,000, and Ottawa, whose G7-inspired support for *Bluenose* was transparent and welcome, paid $210,000. The remainder came from private donations. The 1995 renewal included a new captain, Wayne Walters, grandson of Angus. It also launched the decade of management by Wilfred Moore's *Bluenose II* Preservation Trust, resulting in a period of relative stability and steady performance by the schooner. The trust ran the ship for a decade and raised money for it for several years thereafter. Late in 2012, as it wound up its involvement with *Bluenose*, the trust was able to return more than $500,000 to the province, along with a commercial building in Lunenburg estimated to be worth more than $365,000.

HIT BY A BUS

If *Bluenose* did her job well under the Preservation Trust, the era was not without its speed bumps, not the least of which was an unfortunate brush with the Canadian political scandal of the decade: the Liberal sponsorship debacle. "It wasn't Willie's [Senator Wilfred Moore's] fault," said Peter Kinley, president of the Lunenburg Foundry. "They [the Trust] were side-swiped by a Liberal bus out of Quebec." At the heart of the sponsorship racket was a scam under which large amounts of federal money were paid to advertising agencies for work that was either not done or worth a fraction of what was paid. Among thirty-five contracts for which Quebec police charged and convicted advertising executive Jean Lafleur with defrauding the government of $1.58 million, three were related to *Bluenose II*.

Testimony at the Gomery Commission, which investigated the scandal, indicated that the program spent $3.3 million on projects connected with *Bluenose II* from 1997 to 2002, most of it supporting a Great Lakes tour by the schooner. Among the improprieties, Jean Lafleur was paid a commission of around $30,000 just for sending a federal cheque for $202,800 to the trust to pay for art prints of the schooner. The prints were supplied but both the federal government and Senator Moore claimed to have no idea what happened to them. Senator Moore added that he knew nothing about the commissions paid to Lafleur. In 2005, the year the Gomery Commission issued its first report, the Government of Nova Scotia withdrew responsibility for *Bluenose II* from the Preservation Trust and assigned it to the Lunenburg Marine Museum Society.

No amount of public affection and government money could keep *Bluenose II* safely afloat much longer. The structural rot that had long cursed the schooner changed her profile, slowed her down, and eventually tied her up once more. By 2006 *Bluenose II* was derelict, used sparingly, and spending a lot of her time alongside in Lunenburg.

The inevitable fork in the road came in 2009. In the face of a mounting economic recession, two ideologically disparate Nova Scotia governments—Rodney McDonald's Progressive Conservatives and then Darrell Dexter's New Democrats—had to sign off on the *Bluenose II* renewal project before a single spike could be driven. Not surprisingly, the premiers shared at least one political conviction: there are no votes in sinking *Bluenose*.

Chapter V

SCHOONER TOWN

Rise again, rise again, that her name not be lost

to the knowledge of men.

-Stan Rogers, "The Mary Ellen Carter"

I n the hot summer of 2012 you could take a short and pleasant stroll in Lunenburg, Nova Scotia, and observe the following:

The waterfront premises of one of Canada's most authentic and charming museums, the Fisheries Museum of the Atlantic.

The oldest remaining salt-banking schooner in Canada, the *Theresa E. Connor*, tied by at the museum wharf.

A classic, early steel-hulled side trawler, *Cape Sable*—of the type that put the *Theresa E. Connor* out of business—also tied up alongside.

A 180-foot steel barque, *Picton Castle*, a square-rigged Cape Horner, lying in her homeport.

At one end of a street called Bluenose Drive, you could visit what may be the cleanest public washroom in Canada, its walls a gallery of compact ceramic tiles, all painted by Lunenburg school children in thematic images of the town.

And, as a bonus, at the other end of Bluenose Drive, with a dogleg turn onto Montague Street, you could get an up-close look and take a personal photo of the brand new schooner *Bluenose* under construction.

It may be a minor miracle that Canadian taxpayers, in the middle of the worst economic slump since the 1920s, would countenance spending $16 million on a wooden schooner—one with no apparent mission in life other than to be looked at, no obvious itinerary, and no prospects of lading. It is no small wonder either that a postcard town in rural Nova Scotia, its population half of what it was a century ago, would to be able to produce such a vessel a decade into the twenty-first century. It has been a hundred years since Nova Scotia's heyday of wooden-shipbuilding skills. Today, even the most highly skilled community college grads could not be faulted for not knowing an adze from a spokeshave.

Citizens of other South Shore communities, some secretly sick of hearing about Lunenburg, will acknowledge that the town is not ordinary. Wander around the hilly streets among the old shingled houses with their dormers, mansard roofs, and Lunenburg bumps and you can feel the difference. Lunenburg is a British Colonial showcase. On one level, the entire town is a museum, loaded with maritime artifacts and ruled by ghosts. But Lunenburg also has felt surprisingly modern

PREVIOUS
Lunenburg's vibrant commercial and social past is evoked by the colourful waterfront fishing premises and the British Colonial architecture that have made the town famous. The red building at the far left in this photo is the Fisheries Museum of the Atlantic, where Lunenburg's fishing and mercantile history is treasured and displayed.

and alive in recent times, and especially during the heady days of the *Bluenose II* restoration.

Unlike Gloucester, Lunenburg no longer smells of fish. It smells of maritime commerce, is buried in maritime architecture, and there are boats wherever you look. Lunenburg appears to be both blessed and burdened by its past, and has become a Maritime metaphor for quality, craft skills, and enterprise. But there is a lingering sense as well of a lost yesterday, of a town that peaked long ago.

OLD MEMORIES, OLDER TRUTHS

Lunenburgers have many acknowledged virtues, enterprise and courage prominent among them. Even their vices seem virtuous. Detractors contend that Lunenburg is mostly famous for a degree of thrift that can curdle into parsimony. In the words of one prominent resident of a nearby town: "Lunenburgers: long pockets and short arms!" Today, attempts to keep traditional Lunenburg alive are promoted by the Lunenburg Waterfront Association Inc. The Association lobbied for provincial support of more than $5.5 million to purchase twenty-four buildings and eight wharves after the giant Clearwater Foods operation left town in

2003. The province put up the money, and the properties currently are being managed by a provincial agency, the Waterfront Development Corporation Limited.

As maritime as Lunenburg feels, the town also boasts a space-age dimension. In a world far removed from wooden schooners, a Lunenburg-based manufacturer, Composites Atlantic Ltd., employs more than three hundred designers and producers of advanced composite products for the aeronautics, defence, and space industries. But an ambitious eye to an industrial future does nothing to blind Lunenburg to its maritime past. At least four general histories of Lunenburg remain current in bookstores around the province, and countless other narrowly focused essays and tributes have been written over the years. Lunenburg is one of the most historically connected towns in Atlantic Canada, with a strong awareness of its past and of the relevance of its past to its present and its future.

A well-known historical irony is that Lunenburg, one of the world's most celebrated fishing towns, was founded by farmers. The settlement process was unorthodox to say the least. England, having finally gained firm possession of Acadia—including mainland Nova Scotia—from France in 1763, decided to improve the settlement stock in the key colony, in effect to breed out perceived sloth and indolence. In the early

1750s an aggregation of 1,453 "foreign Protestants" was recruited from Germany, Switzerland, and Montbéliard, a French territory bordering Switzerland. The site chosen to settle those new arrivals was known by its Mi'kmaq name, *Merliguesh* harbour. The name was changed to Lunenburg in honour of King George II, who held the title of Duke of Brunschweig-Lunenburg, a German territory that had been home to many of the new settlers. The German protestant farmers naturally took to farming. But the ocean lapped at their cabbage patches, and the transformation of the Lunenburg area from farming to fishing and shipping began almost immediately.

ST. JOHN'S: A LUNENBURG INCIDENTAL

Lunenburg's devotion to its history seldom has been more evident than it was at the turn of this century when, on October 31, 2001, vandals torched one of the town's most magnificent buildings, the 250-year-old wooden masterpiece, St. John's Anglican Church. The fire devastated the church, leaving half of it in ashes. The Lunenburg parish not only includes many of the county's most powerful citizens, but the venerable church has friends and supporters the world over, many

On October 31, 2001, the 250-year-old St. John's Anglican Church in Lunenburg was set on fire, possibly by Hallowe'en vandals, more than half of it reduced to ashes. St. John's is regarded as one of North America's best examples of Carpenter Gothic architecture. The $6 million restoration of the church foreshadowed, and in many ways complemented, the subsequent reclamation of Bluenose II on the Lunenburg waterfront.

of whom donated to the cause. The ensuing four-year restoration cost $6.3 million. Funding for the restoration included $1 million from the Federal Infrastructure Program, the same fund that has supported the *Bluenose II* restoration project.

Indicative of the Lunenburg approach to the restoration, and perhaps of the Lunenburg way in general, was the attention to the church's decorative painting and art. St. John's was famous for its display of painted stars on the chancel ceiling. An artist was hired to re-paint the stars, but before work commenced astronomer Dr. David Turner of Saint Mary's University was engaged to determine whether or not the stars formed a random pattern. Dr. Turner established that they were not random, and concluded that the 700-star pattern depicts the Lunenburg sky as it would have appeared at sunset on December 24, 1 BC, the traditionally accepted birthdate of Jesus Christ.

For a lucky visitor, a Lunenburg experience in full might include an opportunity to sit in St. John's Anglican Church on an extraordinary winter evening with the Halifax Symphony Orchestra accompanying local singer Lennie Gallant. There are no empty pews. But the mark of the shipwright is everywhere—a forehook here, an afterhook there, great inverted midship bends providing archways to the chancel. If tradesmen can unite land and sea, church and schooner, shipwrights have done so in Lunenburg.

The love of Lunenburgers for their town, and Lunenburg's awareness of its own value, were rewarded in 1995 when the town was made a World Heritage Site by the United Nations. The only other Canadian town so designated is Quebec City.

Lunenburg's claim to *Bluenose*, like the town itself, is a practical matter as well as one of principle and pride.

When the time came in 2010 to rebuild the schooner, only one town was ever in the running. The provincial heritage minister at the time was Percy Paris, and he had no doubt about where *Bluenose* would be rebuilt. On December 18, 2009, he confessed: "My heart says Lunenburg should be the place of choice." No one challenged his decision.

Chapter VI

TOMORROW'S *BLUENOSE*

The more I examine the last living example of the great, two-masted Fishermen Schooner, the greater is my appreciation of the skill, resourcefulness, ingenuity, hardiness and courage of the Maritimers, Newfoundlanders and New Englanders, the men who built and sailed these vessels.

- *L. B. Jenson,* Bluenose II: Saga of the Great Fishing Schooners

A s the restoration of St. John's Anglican Church neared completion, the prospect of rebuilding or restoring *Bluenose II* was all the talk in Lunenburg. A year earlier, Al Hutchinson, a seasoned sales and marketing professional with a business degree from Acadia, had joined Covey Island Boatworks as a partner and general manager. For Hutchinson, one of the big attractions of Covey was the possibility that the company could be involved in a *Bluenose* project, which at that time was only talk.

The province placed a call for proposals based on three options for the rebuild. The first was to build a new *Bluenose* using local lumber, essentially to replicate both previous schooners as closely as possible, and to strengthen the links to traditional Nova Scotia shipbuilding. The second was to build her with mainly

OPPOSITE
The Lunenburg Shipyard Alliance (LSA) brought together three very different Lunenburg County companies. LSA founders and leaders included (left) Al Hutchinson, president of Covey Island Boatworks, (centre) Wade Croft, co-owner of Snyder's Shipyard, and (right) Peter Kinley, president of the Lunenburg Industrial Foundry and Engineering Ltd.

imported hardwoods, in the interest of strength and durability. The final possibility, with similar imperatives, was to build the schooner with composites, wood laminated with epoxy. The third option was straight up Covey Island's street. Covey enjoys an established reputation for turning out large composite vessels. However, as Al Hutchinson notes, when the time came to consider the *Bluenose*, there were obstacles, or at least some tricky considerations.

The province clearly wished to honour Lunenburg's legitimate claim to *Bluenose*. A willingness to build the schooner in Lunenburg became a condition of the "expression of interest" call. Aware of potential blowback from shipbuilders beyond Lunenburg County, the province even had a backup plan to establish a construction site on the Fisheries Museum parking lot in Lunenburg should an outside company emerge as a serious contender.

STRENGTH IN NUMBERS

Covey Island Boatworks is now based in Lunenburg, with additional premises in Riverport, fifteen kilometres south. But given the deeper Lunenburg roots enjoyed by Lunenburg Industrial Foundry and Engineering Ltd.,

Al Hutchinson concluded early that for the *Bluenose* project, his company would be unwise to act alone. The Lunenburg Foundry specializes in systems, refits, and vessel maintenance, but not in wood or composite boat construction. For *Bluenose* purposes, however, the company has critical assets, among them two railway launch platforms for repairing and launching sizeable vessels. It also possesses the tools and know-how to create on-site most of the hundreds of metal, electrical, and plumbing components common to all modern ships.

Another likely and strong competitor for *Bluenose* business was Snyder's Shipyard Limited, headquartered at Dayspring, near Bridgewater, on the banks of the LaHave River, twenty kilometres from Lunenburg. Snyder's also shared the potential liability of being less rooted in Lunenburg than the Foundry. On the other hand it has assets that neither Covey nor the Foundry could offer, including a record of several major and many minor overhauls of *Bluenose II*—repairs tantamount to rebuilding the hull over a couple of decades.

Inside Covey Island, Al Hutchinson proposed a partnership with the Foundry because he knew Foundry president Peter Kinley was already thinking about one, possibly with Snyder's. Hutchinson's business partner John Steele, Covey Island's president at the time, first demurred but later agreed to seek a meeting with Kinley and other Foundry executives. At first the Foundry leaders were slightly taken aback, until they learned that Covey Island had already done significant and valuable work on estimates for various construction options. With the partnership concept at least on the table, it was a shorter step to convince the Foundry to welcome Covey Island. "This project was written for the Lunenburg waterfront," Peter Kinley said. "We got the charter together, and based the project at the Foundry, right here at 53 Falkland Street."

Foundry executives themselves looked after the next step, which was to persuade Philip Snyder that Covey Island could help rather than hurt an eventual bid. According to Philip Snyder, it did not take much convincing: "We felt Snyder's could do the job but we were not interested in doing it alone." Al Hutchinson calls this approach "coopetition."

On January 14, 2010, the Lunenburg Shipyard Alliance (LSA) was officially formed, bringing together two centuries of local shipbuilding and repair experience. With their complementary skill sets and their Lunenburg credentials in order, the LSA companies were solidly positioned and almost unassailable when the province called for expressions of interest in the *Bluenose* project. As the only serious player during that initial phase, the LSA, not surprisingly, was the only contender when the rebuild contract was let on July 8, 2010, following a longish round of bargaining over the details.

CAST IRON COMPANY

If there is an unofficial senior partner in the Lunenburg Shipyard Alliance it is the Lunenburg Foundry. Just west of the Lunenburg town centre, where Bluenose Drive ends at the ceramic-art public washrooms, there sits a cluster of red wooden buildings backing onto some serious wharf space. This is the Foundry's weather-worn waterfront headquarters, Plant I. Plant II is its boat maintenance and launching facility on the opposite end of Bluenose Drive, which sits just metres from the old Smith & Rhuland Shipyard where both the original *Bluenose* and *Bluenose II* were born.

On one of the old, red-shingled buildings that make up the Foundry's Plant I complex is a conspicuous sign that reads *Sherman Whaling Supplies*. Another reads *Nantucket Cordage Company*. Still another advertises *Lubricating and Burning Oils*. What's with those businesses? They are not businesses at all, of course, but props left over from the filming in 2011 of a television mini-series, *Moby Dick*, starring William Hurt as Ahab.

The Foundry stood in for whaling premises in 1850s Nantucket—not that much of a stretch.

The Foundry has been a pillar of the Atlantic shipbuilding and the marine and metal supplies industry since 1891. It built the famous Atlantic single-cylinder—one-lunger—gas engine for small fishing boats, along with Peacock, Cinderella, and Lady Scotia stoves. It still advertises itself as "a day's sail from Newport, R. I.," and closer to Europe than any US port. Peter Kinley is the current Foundry boss, and the company has a strong family base. Peter's son, Joseph, an engineer with the company, represents the fourth generation of Kinleys to have been actively involved with *Bluenose*. Peter himself crewed on *Bluenose II* in 1977.

The spirits of Kinleys past haunt the old buildings. In 1920, when W. H. Dennis was talking up Maritime Rights politics at the Halifax Club, it was Peter's grandfather, John James Kinley, company founder and then mayor of Lunenburg, who suggested that a fishermen's schooner race would be a smart idea. Peter's father, John James "Jim" Kinley, son and namesake of the company founder, was one of Nova Scotia's most accomplished and well-known citizens, a former lieutenant-governor from 1994 to 2000. Jim Kinley grew up with the first *Bluenose* and

Christmas 2010 was a time of celebration for all three LSA companies, and the Foundry staff turned out in force for this photo. The late John James "Jim" Kinley, former Foundry president and former Nova Scotia lieutenant-governor, is the elderly gentleman in the middle of the front row. He passed away on May 1, 2012. To his left is Grace Elizabeth Kinley. Their son, Peter, current Foundry president, is standing (red sweater) directly behind.

knew *Bluenose II* from stem to stern. He passed away at eighty-seven on May 1 of 2012, having lived to see the third *Bluenose* hull take shape.

Six months later, Jim's vacant Foundry office remained as he had left it. Still hanging on the walls were his engineering diplomas (including one from MIT) and countless plaques, awards, testimonials, and photographs. Strewn about were the bric-a-brac and curios of a rich and very public life. "I revered what dad had done," Peter Kinley said. Months after his father's death, Peter was still searching for the right moment, and the heart, to pack up the memories and clear the office out.

If Peter Kinley and his Foundry colleagues have powerful ties to history, they are unbound by them. One of their current works in fact is called the Prometheus Project, for which they have devised a patented two-stage solar concentrator to collect solar energy to melt metals and for other clean energy applications. It is no surprise that the Lunenburg Foundry has a motto, as worthy today as it has been in decades past: "Work hard and do it right."

TRUNNELS AND OAKUM

What the Foundry is to iron, zinc, and bronze, Snyder's Shipyard is to oak and Douglas fir—and now, with

The Snyder's Shipyard crew included (front row, left to right) Scot Tanner, John Penny, Josh Woodworth, Lawrence Verge, and Gordon Slauenwhite; (middle row, left to right at floor level) Nic Hirtle, Rex Rodeniser, Vincent Dorey, and Philip Snyder; (top row, left to right) Wade Croft, Brian Hirtle, Gary Hirtle, Dennis Stewart, and Blaine Alinard.

the *Bluenose* restoration project, to an exotic and rot-resistant South American hardwood: angelique.

Snyder's, located on the eastern banks of the LaHave River, twenty kilometres southwest of Lunenburg town, may be one of the world's best remaining repositories of traditional shipwright skills. Adzes, axes, spokeshaves, and beetling irons are all part of the Snyder's toolkit, as are three of the largest band saws in Canada. Where modern carpenters might favour brads and pneumatic hammers, a Snyder's shipwright is at home with treenails, or "trunnels" (tapered wooden fasteners), and, like pioneering railroad workers, with galvanized spikes driven home in a chorus by iron mallets. It should be noted that "at home with" is a relative phrase. Snyder's

Wade Croft, co-owner with Philip Snyder of Snyder's Shipyard in Dayspring, started as a caulker with the company thirty years ago and worked his way into his current position. Wade is a hands-on boss who frequently pitched in alongside his crew on the Bluenose II *restoration project.*

year of driving oakum, he developed a severe case of "caulking elbow," a condition known to shipwrights long before tennis elbow and centuries before carpal tunnel syndrome. Phillip Snyder and Wade Croft together have seen more *Bluenose II* entrails than most people would care to. Snyder's main *Bluenose II* intervention was the $500,000 repair job in 1994–95 when 60,000 board feet of new lumber went into the schooner, virtually renewing her planking and frames.

HEART OF LAMINATE

The "fusion" company in the Lunenburg Shipyard Alliance is Covey Island Boatworks. Covey Island itself, where the company started in 1979, is one of the LaHave Islands, just south of Bridgewater. John Steele, one of three company founders, still recalls the early days and the struggles of ferrying clumsy band saws and planers to the island on rickety rafts, and trying to convince skeptical fishermen that there might be something to this newfangled wood-lamination-and-epoxy business. From modest cold-moulded canoe and kayak beginnings on the island, Covey has grown into a modern big-boat builder with an international reputation and prestigious achievements.

workers are practical people, too. While they possess the entire traditional kit, they would be no more inclined to use a hand tool where a power tool would lighten the load than they would be to go out and hug a tree.

The senior man at Snyder's is Phillip Snyder, master shipbuilder, son of Teddy Snyder, the original owner. For Phillip, sixty-seven, "semi-retired," as he claims to have been since 2006, means showing up at the shipyard every day in a hard hat and coveralls. His partner is Wade Croft, fifty-two, who has worked his way into co-ownership of the yard over a thirty-year career. Wade describes his job today as "managing the place with Phillip and doing a bit of caulking." Croft actually started at Snyder's as a caulker, or "carker." But after about a

After a decade of growth, Covey moved its expanding operation to a nearby mainland location at Petite Rivière. Soon after, it won a commission to build a unique vessel that would move the company into the international world of large, composite custom yachts. The seventy-foot schooner, *Tree of Life,* was designed by renowned Canadian naval architect Ted Brewer. She was built to go around the world, which she has done twice. In the early 1990s *Sail Magazine* named *Tree of Life* one of the one hundred greatest yachts in North America.

Like *Bluenose II* and St. John's Church in Lunenburg, Covey Island Boatworks is itself something of a phoenix. In 2008 the company's entire Petite Rivière facility was wiped out by fire. Lost in the fire was the yacht *Maggie B,* a Covey-built beauty that had come back to the yard for routine maintenance after a circumnavigation. In 2010, at its new premises in Riverport, Covey Island completed the fifty-eight-foot replacement schooner *Farfarer* for *Maggie B*'s owner, Frank Blair. The vessel exemplified Covey's swift recovery, and *Farfarer* has become another of its signature and internationally known vessels, famous for her articulating and freestanding carbon-fibre masts. Covey's total production now numbers close to a hundred vessels.

By one of the more compelling coincidences of its shipbuilding history, just as most Covey Island employees

Bluenose workers had varied backgrounds. Al Wells, left, is a cabinetmaker from Ontario who had worked for Covey Island on several projects. Douglas "Digger" Leppard, a blue-water sailor, finished up several years of cruising and came home hoping to work on Bluenose. Digger wrote a song about Bluenose, which he performed at the launch. Among the lyrics: "A task more noble there cannot be/Than restoring the Bluenose to the way she ought to be...."

were flat-out busy on the *Bluenose* restoration in October 2011, the company won a contract to outfit a steel-hull replica of *Columbia,* the 1923 *Bluenose* rival, then under construction in Florida. The original *Columbia* had been built specifically to race *Bluenose* for the Fishermen's Trophy, which she did in 1923. The best-of-three series was inconclusive. *Bluenose* clearly outsailed *Columbia* in two races, but the second was awarded to *Columbia* on a technicality. Angus Walters, in full snit, sailed

The core of the Covey Island crew in 2010 included (front row, left to right) Bill Morton, Chris Doherty, Richard Rodenizer, and Colin O'Toole; (back row, left to right) Al Hutchinson, Jeff Robar, Michael Higgins, Rodney Levy, John Steele, Terry Sundbo, Tim Swinamer, and Dave Holmes. Missing Covey Island Boatworks employees: Brian Aulenback, Bo Chambers, Margie Dafoe, Patrick Hirtle, Joel Irving, Johnny Jones, Roy Landis, "Digger" (Doug) Leppard, Danielle McCarthy, Marc McCarthy, Brendan O'Toole, Al Wells, Ronald Young, and Jody Zink.

Bluenose home to Lunenburg, claiming victory based on his two wins. *Columbia's* skipper, Ben Pine, gallantly rejected the organizers' offer to take the trophy by sailing unchallenged around the course. Sadly, the two great schooners never met again.

The steel replica of *Columbia* was built by Brian D'Isunia of Eastern Shipbuilding Group Inc. in Panama City, Florida, from a set of *Columbia* drawings he discovered twenty years earlier. D'Isunia also is known as the builder and original owner of the *Andrea Gail*, the seventy-foot steel trawler that sank with all hands on October 28, 1991, inspiring the book and subsequent movie, *The Perfect Storm*.

The Covey Island commission for the new *Columbia* included all spars and running and standing rigging. Spinning off the Covey Island contract, significant work for *Columbia* found its way to other Lunenburg-area suppliers. Arthur Dauphinee's shop on Second Peninsula near Lunenburg built a hundred or more wooden blocks for the schooner. Standfast Fittings of Blue Rocks fabricated the stainless steel mast fittings, and LaHave Marine Woodworking fashioned the mast hoops. Michele Stevens Sailloft Ltd., half-hour drive along the Second Peninsula from Lunenburg, cut *Columbia's* sails, just as it did for *Bluenose II*.

RED, DARK BLUE, LIGHT BLUE

The *Bluenose* restoration project invited a natural division of labour for the Lunenburg Shipyard Alliance. Covey Island Boatworks, cold-moulding aces, would construct and laminate the frames, keelson, deck beams, and carlings. They would be responsible for the "ceiling"—all the interior hull-coverings below-deck. They also crafted or restored the companionways, cabin accommodations, and deck furniture. And they would rig the schooner. Snyder's would take on the schooner's spine: the keel, sternpost, deadwoods, forefoot, and stem. They would hang the exterior planking and lay the decking. They also would do the caulking. The Lunenburg Foundry was the obvious choice for systems and steel; it would handle all metal components, mechanical and electrical systems, plumbing, hydraulics, and steering. The Foundry would also prepare the site and build the side-transfer platform. And, finally, they would "de-commission," in effect dismantle, the old *Bluenose II*. Each partner would play to its strengths. And when the project is completed each member of the LSA will have *Bluenose II,* one of the world's most recognizable tall ships, as its calling card.

All three partners say the alliance has worked well overall, with each company sticking mainly to its knitting but collaborating readily. The company assignments were

Nova Scotian by birth and Maritime by pedigree, the restored Bluenose II *will fly the Maple Leaf flag and become a Canadian symbol. The new* Bluenose *honours her Canadian status in various ways, including this unique table made from a variety of wood and stone from the provinces and territories, and a gold nugget from the Yukon. The table was built by Colin O'Toole, a thirty-year veteran shipwright with Covey Island Boatworks.*

defined but they were not locked into silos. In photos of the restoration, it is common to see workers in different coloured hard hats—dark blue for Snyder's, red for Covey Island, and light blue for the Foundry—doing the heavy lifting and mucking in as needed.

Colin O'Toole, who at age fifty has worked for Covey Island Boatworks for three decades and is the only remaining shipwright from the company's original shop, regards *Bluenose II* as the project of a lifetime. A skilled woodworker, Colin was given the coveted assignment of creating a unique piece of furniture for the schooner. The fo'c'sle table, eight feet long but eccentrically shaped in width to fit the available space, was made with materials from every Canadian province and territory. Featured are spruce, oak, maple, pine, and walnut; ten pieces of granite from Nunavut to lay hot plates on; a gold nugget from the Yukon, safely sealed into the table under glass, and Acasta Gneiss rock from the Northwest Territories, reputedly four billion years old…give or take a week. O'Toole burned his own name into the table bottom, along with various premiers' names and signatures, including Darrell Dexter's.

Worker pride was a pervasive restoration theme. Wade Croft of Snyder's likes to tell the story of the difference between an expanded work crew he had on a large project a few years ago and his recent *Bluenose* restoration team. "They had completely different approaches to their work. They all wanted to work on *Bluenose*. They all wanted to work hard. They wanted to be part of history." They were, of course, almost all the same people. The difference? Anybody can work on "vessel X." The A-team works on *Bluenose*.

Chapter VII
ANGELIQUE

Q: "Where was that schooner built?"

A: "Built in the woods, up some Nova Scotia creek."

*I*n his exhaustive study of Nova Scotia cargo schooners, *Sails of the Maritimes*, John P. Parker recalls this old sailors' epithet about schooner construction. And it was frequently true: the Nova Scotia shipbuilding era, with peaks and valleys, lasted from the early seventeenth century until the Second World War. The late nineteenth and early twentieth centuries were major periods of fishing-schooner construction, while square-riggers and big cargo schooners were built in vast numbers but in fits and starts through the eighteenth and nineteenth centuries and as late as the 1930s. Entire schooners commonly were cut from mature hardwood and coniferous wood stands that kissed the coastline, or could be found readily up any Nova Scotia creek. Birch and oak provided keels, stems, and sternposts, while spruce and hackmatack (juniper) were deemed ideal for frames and planking.

Well before the age of university educated marine architects there were plenty of Nova Scotians who could build boats. Half-models were carved, typically

The designers recommended white oak from New York State to rebuild the bones of Bluenose II, *but large and seasoned supplies were not readily available. Al Hutchinson of Covey Island Boatworks discovered a small private supply of well-dried angelique in Washington State, which suggested a viable alternative to white oak and enabled an earlier start on construction.*

three-eighths of an inch to the foot in the pre-metric world; "a task not undertaken by an amateur," as John Parker notes. From the half-models, full-scale drawings were sketched on a wooden floor and from these sketches moulds were made for the various sections of the hull. Using the moulds as guides, ribs and frames were fashioned.

While schooners had an increasing presence, the overwhelming majority of vessels built and sailing out of Maritime ports in the late nineteenth century were square-riggers. Their primary business was international trade: lumber and fish to US and Caribbean markets; molasses, rum, salt, and sugar home. Often lost among the impressive square-rigger fleet, the two-masted schooner—with its innovative fore and aft rig—was finding its niche in the salt fishery on the offshore banks. Schooners required smaller crews than the square-riggers, and were more maneuverable in tight coastal and harbour areas. More importantly, for fishing purposes, schooners became increasingly faster as their designs were modified and their rigging was tweaked.

The North American schooner was developed mainly in the United States and worked its way north, many of the building skills arriving in Nova Scotia with United Empire Loyalists who fled the American Revolution. However, Nova Scotia has a fair claim to perfecting the schooner, its potential fully realized in the banking schooner for offshore dory fishing, *Bluenose* being one good example. As schooner development reached full maturity in the early years of the twentieth century, it reflected a gradual shift by the Gloucester fishing fleet away from distant banks salt fishery, towards closer range and quicker trips for fresh fish. This influenced design differences between the Nova Scotia and Massachusetts schooners.

Schooners venturing farther offshore and staying longer, usually to the Grand Banks of Newfoundland and often out of Nova Scotia ports, required increased cargo capacity. They also needed outstanding rough-weather endurance and a good turn of speed. Lunenburg and other Nova Scotia schooners got longer and wider, gaining both speed and stability. Gloucester schooners stayed shorter and were often narrower. They were fast but lighter, and sometimes less seaworthy. While those differences were not always huge—and there were many exceptions—the traits remained apparent during the two decades of Fishermen's Trophy racing, with *Bluenose* often defeating smaller and lighter American vessels. Early Nova Scotia schooners were considered virtually disposable. The combined factors of seasonal fishing, readily available trees, and platoons of skilled shipbuilders made it faster and cheaper to build new schooners than to maintain old ones.

Times and values have changed. It has been fifty years since *Bluenose II* was launched. She remained active, if expensively maintained, for forty-six years, the equivalent of at least three traditional schooner lifetimes. The original *Bluenose*, too, achieved a comparatively long schooner life of twenty-five years. But she sailed, and sank, well past her best-before date. The new *Bluenose*, made from very different materials, will easily last fifty years, and with far less maintenance than with the old *Bluenose II*. That will mean a *Bluenose* schooner will have existed for almost a century and a half.

OLD IDEAS, NEW TECHNIQUES

In wooden-schooner construction, the more things change, the more they are the same. A schooner is still a schooner. And when, like *Bluenose*, a schooner is deliberately designed to replicate a previous one, the differences will lie not in shape and demeanor but in the quality of the construction materials and the techniques. In exterior dimensions, Bluenose Now is the same as *Bluenose II*, which was exactly the same as the original 1921 *Bluenose*. The schooner is 143 feet long and 112 feet on the water line. Her beam is twenty-seven feet and, fully ballasted, her draught will be at least sixteen feet. The running and standing rigging have been remarkably similar for all three vessels.

The critical differences lie elsewhere. The notion is a romantic one of Lunenburg-area shipbuilders of 2011, genetically linked to their forebears of the 1920s, once again picking up their adzes and fashioning the frames for a new *Bluenose* by hand. Reality is more prosaic. The adze and the spokeshave always will have a place in wooden-boat construction, but most modern schooner-building tools need to be plugged in. The idea of the schooner being extensively fastened together with treenails made from local locust wood is also appealing. Here, too, technology has overtaken tradition. Treenails, or "trunnels," are still used in schooner construction, but in the *Bluenose* restoration only sparingly, to help join the sections of frames, and to help fasten frames to the keel. Instead, the fasteners of choice were galvanized spikes, eight inches long by three-eighths of an inch thick—the LSA says 10,798 were used in total—driven into the pre-drilled holes by workers swinging sledgehammers.

Most importantly, while Bluenose Now is a wooden schooner, the dominant wood used, angelique, is different—harder and heavier from that used in her predecessors. The lamination or cold-moulding process for shaping much of the wood was unheard of in the 1920s. Nor was it used for *Bluenose II* in 1963, though it had become more common by then.

In March of 2010, Al Hutchinson of Covey Island Boatworks was in Portland, Maine, attending the Maine Boatbuilders Show. During a discussion with Ted Pike, a writer for *Wooden Boat* magazine, the topic of the *Bluenose* rebuild came up. What was the best material? White oak, primarily from New York State, was the design consultants' choice, but as with many fine

hardwoods these days, there was a catch. A supply of the white oak in quantities and dimensions required for *Bluenose* could take as long as five years to acquire.

Ted Pike had a thought. He knew of a recently deceased sailor, Bill Robinson, of Port Townsend, Washington, who shortly before his death had ordered a supply of a South American hardwood called angelique. He had planned to restore his own wooden yacht, a seventy-foot ketch. Robinson's family was flattered that the two flatbeds of angelique delivered to Bill's home in Washington State would find their way into the restored *Bluenose II*. They felt there was no better place for the wood to go.

Workers at Snyder's Shipyard in Dayspring on the LaHave River had to extend the range of this sliding band saw to mill forty-foot lengths of angelique. The dense hardwood proved difficult to cut, shedding clammy sawdust and destroying saw blades.

South American angelique has been recognized for decades as excellent wood for boatbuilding. As early as 1958, the United States Department of Agriculture and the University of Wisconsin issued a major report on angelique, heralding its durability and strength. The agency reported that angelique trees averaged ninety-five feet in height with diameters of about twenty-four inches. Maximum height was about 150 feet, with some trees five feet in diameter.

Robinson's supply of angelique was nowhere near enough to rebuild *Bluenose*, so it was augmented with another small supply of seasoned angelique located at Vineyard Haven on Martha's Vineyard, which proved helpful in two ways. Firstly, both supplies had aged already for several years, which meant they could be used to build frames and deck beams, where greener wood, more subject to settling and warping as it dries out, is less desirable. And secondly, it moved the production schedule up. Work could start several months earlier than anticipated, and those extra months enabled the Lunenburg Shipyard Alliance to locate larger supplies of angelique from major US suppliers and directly from Suriname in South America. The newer wood could be delivered sufficiently dried for the hull planking, the keel, and other components.

The US report of 1958 did, however, cite certain characteristics of angelique that bedeviled the Snyder's and Covey Island shipwrights five decades later: "After the wood is thoroughly air dried or kiln dried, it can be worked effectively only with carbide-tipped tools. A planer cutting angle of fifteen degrees is said to be suitable for working this species." LSA workers complained constantly about how hard and clammy the angelique was to saw and trim. Saw blades for the *Bluenose* frames alone became a $10,000 expense. On the upside, as the US government report also observed, "the wood finishes smoothly and is moderately easy to glue." The Bluenose Now shipwrights agreed.

The US studies evaluated angelique against competing woods in a variety of other ways, including resistance to abrasion, weathering features, fastening strength, and high silica content—the latter a measure of a wood's resistance to both termites and the unseemly teredo, a tropical, wood-boring clam. The wood received good grades on all fronts. For Bluenose Now, the attractive features of the chosen wood are its strength to resist schooner hogging, and its general resistance to rot. Fortunately for wooden boat lovers, angelique remains available in abundance…up countless Suriname creeks.

Chapter VIII
A KEEL IS STILL A KEEL

Obsolete…what? Are the Southeastern Trades obsolete? Ocean swells—are they obsolete? There's nothing obsolete about a beautifully built, well-balanced schooner.

-*Captain Dan Moreland,* Picton Castle, *2011*

Angelique for Bluenose Now arrived in Dayspring in forty-foot lengths, some of it thick enough to yield pieces two feet square. Snyder's and Covey Island shipwrights milled the wood into a variety of sizes, depending on its use, the damp sawdust clinging to their coveralls and goggles. Some of the biggest pieces needed were twelve inches by twelve inches, thirty or more feet long, destined for the keel. Even at those lengths the keel pieces required scarfs (overlapping tapered joints) to bring them to their full length of more than fifty feet. With the keel in place on the floor of the new aluminum-framed, fabric-covered construction shed in Lunenburg, the remainder of the schooner's spine took shape. Shaping and connecting its components was the job of the Snyder's crew.

The spine or backbone of a schooner starts with the keel and includes components such as the stem, forefoot, and sternpost that extend the keel upward fore and aft.

Angelique is a proven boatbuilding wood that is rot resistant and durable in fresh and salt water. These longer pieces have been milled twelve inches square for sections of the schooner's keel and deadwood.

The Bluenose *keel is relatively short, around fifty feet, but no single piece of angelique could be shipped long enough to span the full length. The keel is a stacked unit four feet high, and the two pieces used to build each layer had to be "scarfed," or joined, their long, tapered ends bolted together. Checking and securing one of the scarfs are Snyders' workers (left to right) Nic Hirtle, Brian Hirtle, Dennis Stewart, and Philip Snyder.*

The completed structure defines a schooner's length and influences the shape and arc of her deck. To form the massive keel, four pieces, each a foot square, were stacked, creating a solid wall four feet high. The pieces were fastened together with galvanized bolts, some as long as five or six feet. To ensure strength at the scarf,

or joint, each piece is tapered to a six-foot-long wedge. These complementary wedges are overlapped, then bolted and glued together to form a unit, as solid as if it had grown that way.

A schooner is a unique vessel in that so much of the hull, both fore and aft, rises out of the water. These sections are called overhangs. *Bluenose* is 143 feet long, but the actual keel is surprisingly short, less than half of her total length. The basic keel of *Bluenose* ends 50 feet or more from the bow. There it yields to a series of gradually curved and scarfed sections that make up the forefoot, the piece that cuts the water as the schooner moves forward. The forefoot rises gently upward to the stem itself, a shorter and more acutely curved piece that defines the final turn and shape of the schooner's bow.

While the keel runs farther aft, the deepest section of the schooner's belly does not run with it. Not far aft of midship, the schooner again narrows and flares gradually upward leaving a large, hollow area, known as the deadwood, between the keel and the rounded bottom of the hull. It is filled in like Lego, with pieces of angelique of varying lengths, all a foot square to match the keel. The deadwood supports the rising stern of the boat, including the overhang, and also contributes to the vessel's stability by adding to the keel's lateral resistance to heeling and to drift. These deadwood

PREVIOUS

Cranes had to be used to move the massive structural pieces into and around the construction shed. Here the pre-assembled forefoot and stem are hoisted in.

LEFT

Movable metal brackets bolted to the floor of Covey Island's plant in Riverport could be adjusted to the exact shape of a given frame, creating a mould. The epoxied laminates were drawn tight against the brackets and left to harden overnight.

CENTRE

The solid frame structure of the restored Bluenose II was achieved by cold-moulding: layers of wood glued with epoxy resin and bent into the correct shapes before the epoxy hardened. The layers, or "lams," for the frames were sawed into pieces eight inches wide and three-eighths of an inch thick.

RIGHT

The lams were drawn into place against the brackets with hand-cranked "come-alongs." In most cases, twenty-one lams were stacked and glued to make up the finished rib, or "futtock." One futtock constituted only half of a frame for one side of the schooner, so four such pieces were needed to make a full, finished frame. Bluenose Now required sixty-two frames in total.

pieces of angelique are stacked and fixed in place with nuts and bolts and drifts, just like the keel pieces. Drifts are metal rods similar to bolts, except that they are embedded like dowels in the adjacent pieces of wood to reinforce the joints.

With the backbone in place and her stern and bow defined, the schooner is ready for the frames. Like the ribs attached to a human backbone, the frames of a schooner shape the hull and provide lateral strength. Creating the frames for Bluenose Now fell primarily to Covey Island workers because of the process used to construct them.

Lamination and cold-moulding are the construction techniques that set this *Bluenose* apart from her predecessors. First used during the Second World War to construct light aircraft, cold-moulding simply involves the gluing together of thin strips or veneers of wood. The thinness of the strips enables bending, and each layer enhances strength and durability. Wood lamination with epoxy effectively creates a new material with eight to nine times the strength-to-weight ratio of steel. It is not susceptible to osmosis, the gradual absorption of dampness, or to separation or delamination. A key advantage of cold-moulding is that it prolongs the life of a wooden boat without dramatically increasing its weight.

THE NEW WAY

For the two previous *Bluenose* schooners the frames were literally sawn and hewn by hand from massive pieces of oak. Cut by cut, shaving by endless shaving, with axes, adzes, spokeshaves, and planes, the frames for a traditional wooden schooner were fashioned to a shape dictated by the wooden half-models and their scaled-up drawings on the loft floor. Covey Island and Snyder's crews sawed thin individual strips for the ribs at the Snyder's yard in Dayspring, which were then were trucked fifteen kilometres to the Covey Island plant in Riverport at the mouth of the LaHave River. Most of the ribs or half-frame sections for Bluenose Now consist of twenty-one veneers, or "lams," of angelique, each eight inches wide and three-eighths of an inch thick.

At the Riverport shed, the lams were stacked on top of each other and bonded with epoxy resin. Bolted into the shed floor are a series of moveable L-shaped metal brackets that could be adjusted to the required shape of a given frame. Once glued together, but while still flexible, the stack of lams would be drawn against those brackets with hand-cranked come-alongs to adhere to the prescribed contour. The bent ribs were then clamped tight and set to dry overnight. Next morning each rib was unclamped and lifted out, rock-solid and perfectly shaped to be fitted side to side with its twin to form a finished frame, sixteen inches wide.

The ribs were manufactured at the rate of four a day, to create one complete set of frames. With sixty-two sets required, creation of the frames alone was a three-month project for the Covey Island team. The solid ribs were trucked another fifteen kilometres from Riverport to the Covey Island shop at the Lunenburg Shipyard. There, the outside edges of each were bevelled to receive the planks. At the nearby boatbuilding site, each pair of ribs was spiked and trunneled together to form the finished frame. Very few structural pieces of a schooner the size of *Bluenose* can be lifted by hand. Completed frames weighed as much as two thousand pounds. They were hoisted by a crane and gently steered into their places on the keel.

For Bluenose Now, the frames, keelson, deck beams, bulkheads, ceiling, the fore and aft deck supports (carlings), and the deckhouse roof are all cold-moulded. The keelson runs fore and aft over the frames and helps seat them into place on the keel. At each frame, bolts five and six feet long run through the keelson, through the base of the frames and all the way down through the keel, fastening all three units together.

The ceiling of a schooner is not like the ceiling of a house. It is the interior liner-covering of the frames, running from the deck all the way down to the finished floor. The new *Bluenose* ceiling is structural, made of four, half-inch-thick, laminated layers of Douglas fir. The ceiling technique is classic cold-moulding, with two of the four strips layered diagonally. It actually forms a

On January 21, 2011, the first finished frame, weighing nearly a ton, was hoisted in to be set on the keel and bolted into place.

As the frames were installed, Bluenose took on the profile of a long-necked skeletal dinosaur. This image illustrates the extraordinary length of the forefoot and stem, and the proximity of the frames to each other. The frames are on twenty-seven-inch centres.

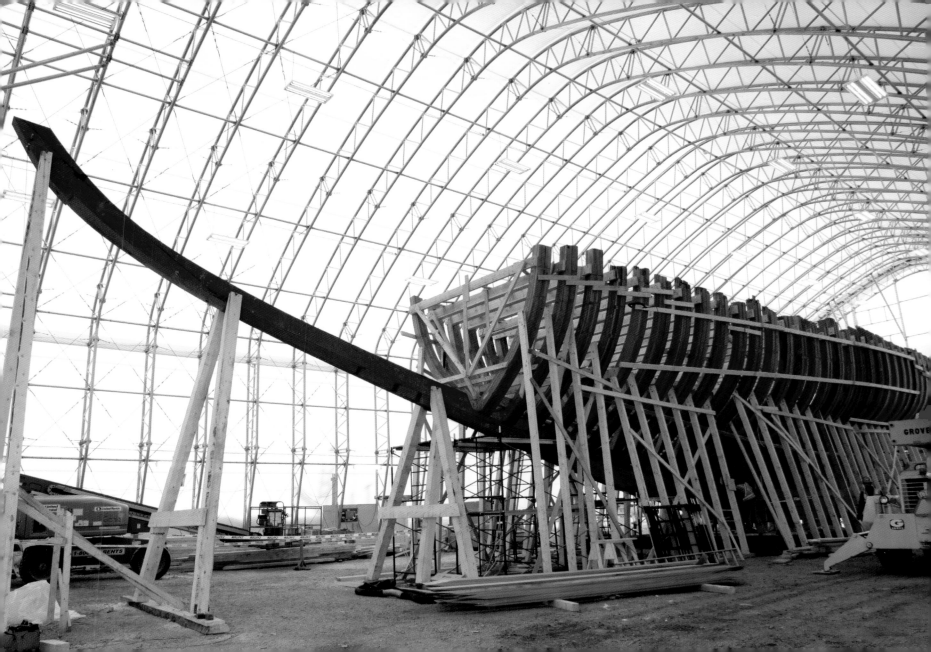

second strong skin for the hull, adding to the schooner's structural strength.

While they are not cold-moulded, the hull planks for Bluenose Now also are cut from the heavy angelique. Each strip, or "strake" to those who speak schooner, ranges from about three inches thick to nearly four for the "garboard strake," the bottom plank that is rabbeted or notched into the keel. Each is five inches wide. Varying in lengths from ten or a dozen feet up to forty feet, they could weigh as much as three hundred pounds each, making it the work of five or six shipwrights to lift and bend them into place.

Bending pieces of angelique three inches thick and five inches wide can be done in various ways. Wedges can be driven between the plank and metal pins in a frame to force the plank upward or downward. Planks can be

TOP

The keelson of a schooner is a heavy wooden structure that rests on top of the keel, strengthening the schooner fore and aft and supporting other components such as ballast and flooring. The keelson of Bluenose Now is eighteen inches high and a foot wide, and was laminated in place, becoming part of the cold-moulded interior structure.

BOTTOM

The "ceiling" of Bluenose Now

clamped to frames and drawn inward. Occasionally, the planks are steamed hot to make them more pliant. These techniques work for all but one plank on each side of the schooner. Traditionally, one of these planks is declared be the "whisky plank," the last to be installed. This final plank cannot be clamped in place because it closes the last opening in the hull, leaving no exposed frame on which to attach the clamp. The whiskey plank must be cut to fit precisely. The term has exactly the origins you might imagine. When the last spike is driven, a horn of whiskey has been well and truly earned.

Running the entire distance fore and aft inside the schooner is a laminated shelf of Douglas fir, two feet wide, eighteen inches thick. Fixed just below deck level, the shelf is moulded into place and supported by twenty pairs of steel "hanging knees," each two and a half feet high. The shelf supports the beams that run across the ship—"athwart the ship" in schooner-speak. These beams are arced slightly to give the deck a camber that carries water to one side or the other and out the scuppers, the drainage slots in the bulwarks. In turn the beams support the carlings, or "carlins," shorter fore and aft beams that create a grid to help support the deck planks. Also supporting the deck are eighty-five steel "lodging knees," two hundred pounds each. The deck planking itself is three-inch-thick Douglas fir of varying widths, all with

The hull planks, made of angelique

vertical grain: "wood to die for," in the words of LSA project manager Wilson Fitt. The placing of the beams follows the sheer of the schooner. The sheer line makes the deck of a schooner concave fore and aft but flatter in the middle. The sheer and camber of the schooner's deck combine to keep water flowing, out one side or the other, as the schooner rolls and pitches.

KEEPING THE OCEAN OUT

Both the hull and the deck planking of a wooden vessel must be completely watertight. And no matter how tightly the planks are butted or clamped together, their seams will leak if they are not tightly caulked. On *Bluenose* there are more than eighteen kilometres of

The robust deck structure includes arced beams of laminated angelique running athwart the schooner. The carlings ("carlins") running fore and aft between the beams create a heavy grid to support the deck planks and deck equipment. Seventy-five steel "lodging knees" were custom-built by the Foundry and installed as structural supports, while the deck planking itself is Douglas fir, three and a half inches thick, with vertical grain.

seams. This enormous caulking job fell to the Snyder's crew. Snyder's man Rex Rodenheiser, who did the lion's share of the caulking, spent nearly three months on scaffolds or on his knees, contributing mightily to the back-breaking task.

The methods and materials for caulking a schooner are traditional. The main waterproofing ingredient is an ancient oily product known as oakum. Oakum was once made from discarded strands of rope, soaked in tar. The modern product is oiled hemp. One apocryphal restoration story is that a younger worker could not resist rolling one up to assess the quality of the hemp.

The seams of a schooner actually get worked several times over to ensure tightness. The seams are first stuffed with two strands of cotton and then with one strand of oakum. The oakum strand is "horsed" or cinched in, using chisel-like iron blades called caulking irons, and wooden mallets. The second layer of oakum is then caulked in and "made back," or seated firmly in place. The seams then are "faired" or sanded smooth, and primed with paint. A sealing compound is applied, then more fairing to make the surface ready for finishing. The schooner's hull takes one coat of white primer paint and two coats of the distinctive *Bluenose* black paint. The deck planks are stained.

In the long caulking process, the cotton and oakum are seated home inch by dreary inch: *tap-tap-tap* in the deck seams with the hand irons and smaller mallets, *bang-bang-bang* on the hull with the long-handled horsing mallets, called beetles, and caulking irons. Caulking is the process that has changed least in the ninety-one years from *Bluenose* to *Bluenose* to *Bluenose*.

There are no electric caulking tools; it is all manual work using hand tools, as it has been since the Book of Genesis.

On the original *Bluenose* the final sealant would have been a boiled, gluey soup known as "pitch," a distillation of tar and turpentine. The act of applying pitch to the seams of a wooden vessel is called "paying." The seam at deck level, the longest in the boat, traditionally is called "the devil." The everyday expression, "the devil to pay" has various etymological sources. One of them is a contraction of an even older shipbuilding expression, "the devil to pay and no pitch hot," clearly a more serious predicament than merely "the devil to pay." No pitch hot or cold was required for Bluenose Now. The devil and all other hull seams were paid with modern polyurethane compounds called Sika 290 and 291.

The easiest way to grasp the overall construction concept for Bluenose Now is to imagine a second unified and rigid boat, cold-moulded, built inside an exterior wooden boat formed by the hull planks and the decking. Not only is this cold-moulded inner dermis stronger by weight than steel, it also is divided fore and aft into watertight compartments formed by six leak-proof bulkheads. In short, the new *Bluenose* is by far the strongest banking schooner ever built in Lunenburg. Before she could hog, she actually would have to break— not impossible, perhaps, but an improbable occurrence, if

TOP
Caulking—making the deck and hull of a wooden vessel watertight—has changed very little over centuries. The standard tools are caulking irons and mallets, and the standard tightening materials are strands of cotton followed by two runs of an oily hemp product called oakum.

BOTTOM
Caulking the hull and deck of Bluenose *was a journey that went on for months. Snyders' workers covered an estimated eighteen kilometres of seams.*

One change in the caulking process is that chemical sealants have replaced boiled tar or "pitch" to cover the caulked seams. The care and patience required is indicated by the masking tape used to ensure the black gunk did not soil the newly sanded deck planks. The inevitable wear and tear on the knees and other joints of the "carkers" is suggested by the kneeling and crouching contortions of Dennis Stewart, left, and Brian Hirtle.

her length can be altered. Her sheer, however, can be adjusted, which could affect her appearance and possibly even her performance.

The sheer of a boat is the gradual curve fore and aft of her topsides. The sheer of *Bluenose*s past and present is not a minor topic. Schooner buffs debate it the way theologians discuss original sin. The high *Bluenose* bow is an unusual schooner feature. It sweeps up more abruptly than the gentler arc from her stern to her foremast might logically dictate. In the eyes of many, this more prominent bow detracts from the schooner's grace. But admirers swear it has made *Bluenose* look more competent and aggressive, and may have even made her faster.

PIPES, CABLES, AND SPARS

In October of 2012, *Bluenose* lay alongside the Foundry's Plant I wharf in Lunenburg, swarmed by workers from all three LSA crews.

Covey Island was responsible for stepping the masts and installing the rigging, all salvaged from *Bluenose II*. The *Bluenose II* masts are of two generations. The foremast, a solid piece of Douglas fir, is from the mid-1990s and is due for replacement in a year or two. It stands seventy-two feet above the deck, and carries a

the schooner can avoid unfriendly encounters with rocks and icebergs.

When the backbone and frames are in place, a schooner is defined and can be fully imagined in her three-dimensional form. At that point, in terms of overall shape, a schooner is what she is. Neither her width nor

topmast of fifty feet. The mainmast stands eighty-three feet above deck and its topmast adds another fifty-two feet. This mainmast was replaced in 2007, is of laminated Douglas fir, and is in top shape. According to former skipper and current *Bluenose* operations manager Wayne Walters, the big advantage of a laminated mast is "you know what's in the middle."

A Snyder's crew was completing exterior carpentry and deck work. The Foundry team, meanwhile, was tackling some tough jobs too: wiring, metal fittings such as windlasses, and especially the stainless steel rudder. The Foundry's shop crew manufactured the water piping and conduits for wiring, exhaust, and air conditioning, and a variety of stainless steel water and fuel tanks.

By mid-summer 2012 foundry plumber Richard Hodder had already spent about nine months below decks on *Bluenose* running pipe for five washrooms with showers plus all lines for the galley. Richard was undeterred. "Every moment is a proud one," he told *Herald* reporter Beverly Ware at the time.

Bluenose's twin 235-horsepower John Deere diesels had been installed before the launch. Many of the systems, such as electrical and plumbing, had also been started earlier but now had to be fitted into designated slots, as Covey Island workers completed below-decks furnishings and cabinetry.

The electrical system became a challenge because of the demand for materials not readily available. Electrical components for both aircraft and ships have had to meet much more stringent standards and inspections in the past decade or so. According to Peter Kinley of the Foundry, the increased rigour is in part a product of a Nova Scotia tragedy, the crash of Swissair Fight 111 near Peggy's Cove in 1999, attributed to faulty wiring.

Many of the men and women who built the new schooner are direct descendants of the men who built the original. They practiced crafts in common with their forefathers, and the final creation of their work looks remarkably similar to theirs.

If there is a First Family of Bluenose construction, it is the Hirtles. Four generations of the family have worked on *Bluenose* schooners. Clifford "Cliffy" Hirtle was born in Dayspring in the late 1880s and worked on the first *Bluenose* in 1921. In 1963 his son Warren was a shipwright with the Smith & Rhuland Shipyard, and worked on *Bluenose II*. Gary and Brian, Warren's sons, are long-time members of Snyder's core team, and both have been with the *Bluenose* restoration project throughout. Gary's son, Jason, meanwhile, works for the Foundry.

PREVIOUS

Following the launch of the new Bluenose II *hull on September 29, 2012, the schooner was tied up to a Foundry dock at the opposite end of the Lunenburg waterfront. There, the many salvaged components of the old schooner were rehabilitated and installed, the plumbing and electrical systems completed, and the masts stepped.*

Chapter IX

BUREAUCRACY, BUCKS, AND WHARF-TALK

Money don't talk, it swears.

-Bob Dylan, 1965

A common enemy can be a unifying force. There was certainly shared frustration for the Lunenburg Shipyard Alliance in doing business with governments and their agencies. Government players, in turn, expressed impatience with the companies and occasionally with each other. It was not surprising that provincial government bureaucrats were not instant experts on building schooners, nor was it surprising that they relied on consultants for whom banking schooners were not exactly routine assignments. While the companies worried about slow government decision-making and frequent changes, the provincial position is that the companies were slow in the early construction phase. Inflexible federal funding deadlines did not help, either.

On one level the frustration of each side reflected the usual ideological tension between governments, whose natural bent is to ponder and plan, and impatient business people whose focus is on the calendar and the

A side-transfer platform, on which the schooner sits, was part of the overall project and had to be installed before construction of the new schooner could begin. There are three rolling cradles on which vessels can be built and then mechanically cranked sideways to an existing rolling platform (foreground), which rolls in the opposite direction for launching.

There have been legitimate differences of opinion in the mix, and some honest concerns expressed about the schooner herself. While the Nova Scotia government has spoken freely about many of the issues, the companies directly involved in the *Bluenose* rebuild were obliged to sign non-disclosure and confidentiality agreements. Dear to most governments these days, these agreements are modern gag orders, in effect created at the behest of public officials to hide details of public business from public scrutiny. But if the *Bluenose* contractors themselves were constrained, their grievances were not difficult to detect. As one sage Lunenburger commented, "you could hear it all at Tim's."

FUNDING HIGHS AND LOWS

Most major points of contention ultimately involved money. There is at least $16 million on the table—not

ABOVE

The old schooner, minus her bowsprit, approaches dry dock for the last time in August of 2010. By early 2013 the restoration of Bluenose II *had been in the works for well over three years. Forgotten by many critics were the extensive preparations, including the dismantling of the original* Bluenose II, *and the salvaging of reusable components.*

bottom line. On another level, the unique nature of the restoration project bred its own peculiar challenges. As comedian Stephen Colbert might say, there was "truthiness" in all positions.

Three levels of government have had a voice and a hand in the *Bluenose* restoration project. Three competitive companies have collaborated to build the boat. Dozens of other businesses competed to supply goods and services. The BlackBerries alone would sink a schooner. Then there was and is the dynamic of public scrutiny and opinion. All Nova Scotians rightly claim a piece of *Bluenose*. Their collective local schooner knowledge, or confident opinion, may equal that of the rest of the planet combined. Needless to say, there has been much conjecture and loose chatter. Captain Phil Watson of *Bluenose II* calls it "wharf talk."

a massive amount in the age of government budgetary billions, but not a drop in the bucket, either. A legitimate concern about *Bluenose* costs was whether or not the potential federal stimulus funding could be maximized. Unlike other money issues, the loss of federal funding can be quantified. Ottawa has put less than $5 million into the *Bluenose* restoration. If the schooner could have been built a little earlier, there would have been at least $7 million in and possibly more.

The original cost estimate for the restoration was $14.2 million, half of which the province expected from Ottawa. Indeed, in January 2009, and again on April 30, 2009, Ottawa announced federal funding for the *Bluenose* project at $7.1 million, half of the total projected cost at the time. There were no apparent strings attached.

In August of 2009 the province acknowledged that the cost had gone up half a million dollars to $14.7 million, and by summer of 2012 to an estimated $16 million. The federal share, however, had dropped to $4.9 million. The explanation was that Ottawa had imposed a project completion deadline of March 2011, after which *Bluenose* work could no longer qualify for federal matching dollars. That deadline was later extended to October 2011, but was still beyond reach. The federal rules of engagement not only frustrated the province but also placed the builders in the awkward situation of appearing to miss important deadlines that were impossible to meet in the first place.

On a spring-like day in January of 2013, Bill Greenlaw, the senior provincial government official responsible for the *Bluenose* project, was fighting the flu while temporarily holed up a vacant office in the Maritime Museum of the Atlantic, the door held ajar by a cannonball.

Bill Greenlaw has been conscious of the importance of *Bluenose* since he was about seven. Living in Ottawa at the time, his mother commissioned a painting of a schooner to remind her family of their Nova Scotia home, to which they were determined to return. The schooner was generic, but Bill Greenlaw always thought of it as *Bluenose*. The image captured his imagination.

"It's not untypical to have disputes between builders and owners about who will pay for what; what's in the scope of the contract and what's not," Greenlaw acknowledged. In theory, from the initial federal funding commitment to the funding deadline, the province and the builders could have had two and a half years to complete the project. On the surface, this would appear adequate. Unfortunately it was not that simple.

In fact much work was completed by October 2011, and in the end that work is what leveraged just under $5 million from Ottawa. Could additional work have been

To enable all-weather construction, an aluminum frame and vinyl-clad, heated shed had to be built—large enough for a schooner, several cranes, scaffolding, and a series of temporary workshops. The shed was set up just metres from the old Smith and Rhuland Shipyard premises from which Bluenose *emerged in 1921 and* Bluenose II *in 1963.*

completed to trigger more federal support? Despite its own frustrations with Ottawa, the province takes the position that the builders were slow off the mark. "We couldn't get the builder to build any faster, to present enough invoices," Bill Greenlaw said. In fact there were delays, at least some of them unavoidable. Others may reflect on all the parties involved.

Initially, there were major materials supply issues. John Steele and Al Hutchinson of Covey Island said that the single biggest challenge in building the schooner was sourcing materials. US and Canadian hardwoods were ruled out, unavailable in the dimensions and quantity required, too small, or inadequately seasoned. Additionally, there were design uncertainties and delays, and unanticipated regulatory requirements. Then, only two months after the federal funding announcement, a provincial election and a change of government intervened. Darrell Dexter's NDP government was elected in June 2009. Its commitment to *Bluenose* was anyone's guess, and its support was not confirmed publicly until September of that year.

With the government change, it was December of 2009 before a designer was announced. And while the LSA was created in January of 2010, the actual building contract for *Bluenose* was not in place until July of that year. At that point the first "sunset" deadline for federal

funding was only eight months away; the extended deadline, fifteen months. It is not surprising that the government would wish to blame the builders for delays, and that the builders would wish to deflect responsibility back to government. This is not untypical either.

DRAMA BEYOND THE BOAT YARD

On December 18, 2009, Percy Paris, the new NDP minister of Communities, Culture and Heritage, announced a series of commitments that finally made the project real, but left it well behind the required schedule for federal funding. Less money from Ottawa meant more from Halifax. "Right now we don't know how much it's going to cost," Paris said. "But one of the things that we want to ensure and we want to feel safe in saying is that if we come across any cost overruns we feel confident that there's going to be enough money here that's going to look after them." The schooner is a specialty item, said Paris. "You just can't walk into any store and get [it] off a shelf. A lot of this is going to be handmade."

On the same date the minister announced that the government had chosen the firm of MHPM Project Managers Inc. to manage the *Bluenose* rebuild project,

and Lengkeek Vessel Engineering Inc. as the project's design consultants. The appointment of the latter had its own interesting fallout. The province mandated Lengkeek to design a schooner that would last half a century without major maintenance, and would not hog. Lengkeek of course complied, designing a boat that, among other money-is-no-object features, would have had bronze floors, strapping, and knees, and a consequent price tag well beyond the early estimate of $14.4 million. This design could not happen; it had to be modified to at least approximate the budget.

The province then made a second major decision that has had a financial impact on the *Bluenose* project, the magnitude of which may not be determined until well after Bluenose Now sets sail. It decided that Bluenose Now must be "taken into class," which means meeting the safety and construction standards of one of world's biggest ship classification societies, the American Bureau of Shipping. Transport Canada had advised the province of its movement away from ship inspections, both those under construction as well as ongoing safety inspections. It now delegates its inspection and standards authority to one of five approved private classification agencies. The province chose ABS because the agency maintains an inspector in Nova Scotia. The province has acknowledged that ABS was engaged after the schooner had been designed, but initially denied that there have been major cost increases as a result. Bill Greenlaw had insisted this part of the process had driven only "marginal extra expense." By March of 2013 the provincial minister of

The Bluenose II *design by Lengkeek Vessel Engineering and the enforcement of safety standards by the ship classification society, American Bureau of Shipping, meant delays and modifications as the work progressed. The impressive but often expensive safety requirements included the virtually bulletproof glass in ports (left) and watertight bulkheads (right).*

Communities, Culture and Heritage was acknowledging cost increases driven by regulatory demands, in amounts still unspecified.

According to Bill Greenlaw, the business of taking *Bluenose* into class, or "classing," has been widely misunderstood, even in ship-literate Lunenburg. In effect, Greenlaw says, "ABS *is* Transport Canada. They became the delegated regulator. ABS ensures the vessel is built to Transport Canada standards so that she can be registered as a Canadian vessel and carry the Canadian flag." There are two levels to the services provided by ABS, Greenlaw says. The process of classing is separate from the regulatory authority delegated to ABS by Transport Canada. Greenlaw describes classing itself as a premium service supplied by the agency, above and beyond meeting the usual Transport Canada safety standards. This service ensures materials and systems going into the boat are properly documented, are from reliable manufacturers, and are genuine. The agency ensures that there will be regular inspections and that the crew is certified.

A key advantage of a classed vessel is certification for insurance and liability purposes. Greenlaw was up front about the government's thinking behind this move. "If something ever happened, the first question to the premier would be: 'Why wasn't she taken into class?'"

Events in the years leading up to and during construction of Bluenose Now only increased the government's concern. Tall ships were not getting good press.

On February 17, 2010, *Concordia*, a steel hulled, 188-foot sail-training barquentine familiar to Nova Scotia ports, sank 550 kilometres off Brazil after being hit by a "microburst," a fierce downdraft of wind and rain that laid her down on her beam ends. All sixty-four crewmembers were rescued after enduring thirty hours in life rafts, but the sinking raised questions about *Concordia*'s stability.

More than four years earlier, on December 8, 2006, a tragedy involving another restored tall ship also hit home in Canada, and hit Lunenburg directly. The eighty-year-old barque, *Picton Castle*, an education and training vessel, is registered in the Pacific Cook Islands but based in Lunenburg. The *Picton Castle* was at sea in a storm on a voyage to Grenada that December night when twenty-five-year-old Laura Gainey, daughter of the former Montreal Canadiens hockey player and executive Bob Gainey, was swept over the rail and never seen again. Safety standards on the *Picton Castle* were criticized at the time, as was the vessel's late-season departure from Lunenburg. The *Picton Castle* docks in Lunenburg for several months each year. Her captain, Daniel Moreland, is a respected local resident who defends his vessel and has spoken openly about the incident, insisting he complied with all safety recommendations from Transport Canada before and after the accident.

Then, exactly a month after the launch of Bluenose Now, the venerable HMS *Bounty* went down. The loss not only hit Lunenburg hard, it made the province's safety concerns for the new *Bluenose* look prudent, if not prophetic. In the weeks following *Bounty*'s loss, the region was rife with questions about her stability, overall condition, and general safety features. The decision of her master to try to dodge the path of the well-forecasted Superstorm Sandy has been roundly criticized by many, including Daniel Moreland of the *Picton Castle*.

TALE OF A RUDDER

There can be no quarrel with improved safety standards. But a key problem for the builders was the fact that they signed the building contract at the province's behest before the design was completed and before ABS was engaged. Inevitably, both factors could and did drive changes and cost increases. If the debate needed a focal point for public engagement, and to generate considerable wharf talk, it soon found one: the *Bluenose* rudder.

On the floor of a Lunenburg Foundry metal shop in November of 2012 sat a metal monster of impressive aspect. The rudder is a work of art. Indeed, leaving aside the headaches it created, the Foundry metalworkers should be very proud of it. The upper stock of the new *Bluenose* rudder is a solid twelve-inch-diameter piece of metal, 316-guage stainless steel, a strong and anti-corrosive material. It is about twelve feet long. The huge rudder blade is attached to it by nuts and bolts set through two massive cylindrical steel flanges. The blade itself is fifteen feet high and six feet at its widest. This lower section is made of what is known as "mild steel," a slightly softer grade, though not exactly flimsy.

The foundry's Peter Kinley, a peaceful man, was agitated and mildly annoyed. The *Bluenose* rudder, required by the designer and ultimately requiring ABS approval, was his company's responsibility and in many ways Peter's nightmare. The rudders of previous *Bluenose*s were constructed of massive spruce planks, fastened together by iron rods and straps and light enough to achieve "neutral buoyancy;" to float. However, a steel rudder for Bluenose Now was in the Lengkeek design, and ABS, the enforcer of all standards for the ship, insisted it be built as prescribed.

The frustrations about the rudder were twofold. Firstly, the steel had to be manufactured in ABS-approved

trials would tell the final tale. Increased costs were not quantified, but with manpower, machinery, and metal all considered, the *Bluenose* rudder is estimated to be worth $100,000, an amount worth arguing about.

BALLASTING ACT

A second *Bluenose II* design issue, again hotly debated both on and off the wharf was, ironically, a by-product of the decision to build a stronger schooner. The angelique, the cold-moulding process itself, and the many steel components had added significantly to the weight of the schooner even before ballast was installed. A key objective in any sailing vessel is to place as much ballast as possible as deeply as possible in order to push the centre of gravity down. This ballast, along with other key variables such as the actual shape of the hull, is what enables a sailing vessel to heel safely and sail more efficiently to windward.

One schooner expert has estimated that the centre of gravity on Bluenose Now is higher than it was on *Bluenose II* by as much as four and a half feet. The new schooner will draw more water, perhaps an extra foot. Former *Bluenose II* skipper Don Barr reckons this could make a difference when the vessel is under press of sail,

The new schooner, built of dense angelique and with extensive steel reinforcements, is heavier than her predecessor, and this generated much conjecture regarding stability. In theory, the extra weight is offset by reduced ballast set lower in the hull.

mills, a slow process. By November 2012 the rudder had gone through several iterations, some of them to correct defects as seemingly minor as welds made too close to the nuts and bolts. The second rudder issue was weight, a matter debated by both schooner experts and wharf commentators alike. The 7,500-pound bauble would hang outboard from the very tail end of the schooner. Its tremendous weight raised the question of whether a human being at the wheel end of a mechanical worm-gear steering system would ever be able to turn it.

By the end of January 2013, a warp in the blade had been corrected and the rudder had been approved. Sea

although this does not mean there would be a safety issue. "We were always very comfortable sailing with her scuppers in the water, heeled at twelve or fifteen degrees," Barr says. "The same amount of sail on the new boat might put her top rails in the water."

Much depends on how a new schooner is used. Captain Phil Watson says *Bluenose II* rarely carried her full suit of sails, including topsails, and never in heavy weather. Unlike Angus Walters's *Bluenose, Bluenose II* was neither racing for the Fishermen's Trophy nor was she trying to make it back to Lunenburg to get the best price for salt fish. "Getting *Bluenose* fully rigged and doing fourteen or fifteen knots in a blow is the easy part," says Phil Watson. "Getting her to slow down is harder. I'm not going to be sending young kids aloft to take in topsails in a gale unless we've been caught out and it is absolutely necessary."

It may be years before we know with certainty how Bluenose Now will perform under sail and under stress, and just as long before we know how much of the wharf talk was prophecy. Meantime, there are important consolations. Cost and rudder squabbles notwithstanding, Bluenose Now has emerged from the yard as a remarkable piece of work, its restoration monitored online by thousands of people the world over, its appeal already clearly established, and its arrival warmly welcomed. Overall, throughout the project, general goodwill prevailed, among the LSA partners and with government. Design details were tweaked often, and while the ABS remained constantly vigilant, the builders responded to the demands. For its part, the province remained confident that public support for the *Bluenose* rescue would trump the issue of costs. So far it has.

Chapter X
CAPTAINS COURAGEOUS— AND CHARISMATIC

One mainmast. One skipper.

-A captain's creed

When [Angus] said "move" today, he didn't mean tomorrow.

-Captain Rollie Knickle

By 1980 *Bluenose II* was seventeen years old, almost as old as the original *Bluenose* was when she defended the Fishermen's Trophy for the final time in 1938. If anything, *Bluenose II*, hull for hull, was in sorrier shape at seventeen than Angus's *Bluenose* had been at twenty-five. Under new and untested political masters, *Bluenose II* sailed on, bloodied but unbowed. Political uncertainty was only one challenge. By the 1970s finding able skippers for wooden sailing schooners proved no easier than finding perfect politicians.

Different ships, different long splices. This ancient mariners' rule can be as readily applied to captains as to knots and splices. Angus Walters lived in a day when, if few schooner captains were his equal, experienced and competent skippers were not too hard to come by. This was especially true during the 1920s when the value

OPPOSITE
Captain Angus Walters bears down on the Bluenose *helm during the 1921 local elimination races, in which* Bluenose *had to outsail seven local contenders before she could move on to the International Fishermen's Trophy race. In the big show she recaptured the cup won by* Esperanto *of Gloucester, under Captain Marty Welch of Digby, Nova Scotia, the previous year—before* Bluenose *existed.*

In enemy territory for the 1922 Fishermen's Trophy race, Captain Angus steps out in Gloucester wearing a smart overcoat and an air of confidence. Schooner captains were plentiful in the 1920s, although few had Angus's savvy as a fishing skipper, or as a helmsman in a race or in a gale.

of schooners as fishing vessels was in serious decline. By 1963, when *Bluenose II* slid into a much different Lunenburg harbour from that which had welcomed Angus's *Bluenose*, there were few remaining schooners and even fewer remaining captains.

Most of the diehard banking schooner owners and skippers had called it quits long before. In the 1960s the *Theresa E. Connor*, last of the active bankers (now nicely restored at the Fisheries Museum of the Atlantic in Lunenburg) was unable to find crewmen willing to take to the dories. She sailed to Newfoundland seeking hands and returned to Lunenburg without a single recruit.

ANGUS'S LONG SHADOW

As early as the 1920s, many Nova Scotia fishing masters and schooner owners had been predicting a devastating impact on codfish stocks by the new diesel-powered trawlers. By the early 1960s those prescient laments had been silenced as naïve and self-interested. Money swore louder than ever. The fifty-year pillage of the Grand Banks was well underway. The second half of the twentieth century proved to be a benighted era when diminishing fish stocks were offset by ever-increasing fish prices and expanding catch quotas, an obvious formula for disaster.

Like every ship on every ocean, the success of *Bluenose II* relied largely on the skill and disposition of her captain. The casting of a captain is a complicated matter, and is very much a function of the purpose and mission of the ship. Indisputably, Angus Walters was an exemplary master, up to a point. In the 1935 mid-Atlantic hurricane that pounded and threatened a leaky *Bluenose* on a voyage back from England, Angus would have been your man. Then there was that wild April night in 1926 when Angus was credited with superhuman helmsmanship, saving *Bluenose* from a Sable Island sandbar. Even in friendlier seas, at the wheel of *Bluenose* in a spirited Fishermen's Race, who else to have in command than a bugger to carry sail who claimed his schooner spoke to him?

It is impossible to explore the story of *Bluenose* or her captains without drifting in and out of Angus Walters's shadow. For better or worse, Angus remains the standard by which subsequent *Bluenose* captains are measured. Surprisingly, Angus often lives in *Bluenose* literature and lore as a one-dimensional curmudgeon, a cranky but gifted sailing master. It is not surprising that he is portrayed that way by US schooner historians: "An aggressive, unsportsmanlike and abusive man, but a prime sailor," according to Howard Chapelle, a leading American schooner writer. While this portrait would

have delighted Angus's Gloucester antagonists, it is less than complete. Perhaps by being tied overwhelmingly to schooner racing, Angus and his many other dimensions and achievements were devalued or even distorted.

Angus Walters went to sea in 1895 in typical early twentieth-century fashion: at thirteen he joined his father's schooner, *Nyanza*, as a "flunky." By his mid-teens he was an experienced doryman. By his late teens he had sailed to the West Indies as mate on a schooner with his older brother, John "Sonny" Walters, as skipper. On that voyage, standing right next to Angus in a hard blow, Sonny was carried overboard by a rogue wave. His oilskins filled with water, helping to keep him afloat. Angus took the wheel of the schooner himself and sent two men over the side in a dory. Miraculously, they found Sonny alive and hauled him aboard. Each man received a five-dollar gold piece and a watch for saving the skipper.

Angus was shipwrecked while still in his teens. His father, Captain Elias, was taking *Nyanza* into the Magdalen Islands when she was stove in by ice and sank two miles from shore. Angus and Elias boarded the last dory to leave the schooner. All hands got off and were soon picked up by other nearby vessels. In *Bluenose Skipper*, Walters's biographer G. J. Gillespie captures the romanticized flavour of Angus's probationary schooner years with brief sketches of the young sailor's mentors.

Angus was "broken in the right way." There was able and canny Cap'n Elias to teach him, but other fishing skippers like Cap'n Jimmy "Old Toxy" Hirtle, a gruff salt with an acid tongue, who sailed by the stars and put his faith in the Bible; Cap'n "Long Albert" Himmelman, whose crews claimed he would spit over the lee rail and tell his dorymen to get out the gear 'cuz there's fish here or my name ain't "Long Albert" Himmelman; then there was Cap'n "Old Dit" Young who "pulley-hauled" his schooner home from sea with tackles on the rudder when a mighty sea snapped the rudder chain and left his vessel drifting helplessly in the teeth of a roaring Atlantic gale….

At twenty-six, Angus had held his Master's ticket for three years, and had commanded one schooner, the *Minnie M. Cook*. By then he was sufficiently established as a competent captain and businessman to sell shares in his own banking schooner, then under construction at the Smith & Rhuland Shipyard in Lunenburg. The new vessel was named for his sister, Murial B. Walters. His first trip on the *Murial B.* was as a transatlantic charter to Gibraltar and on to a series of Mediterranean ports. Angus fished in the *Murial B.* for eight years, including the first two years of the First World War.

German U-boats sank ship after ship in Canadian waters, among them a salt banker near the mouth of the LaHave River.

Between 1916 and *Bluenose* in 1921, Angus briefly owned the schooner *Donald Silver*, after which he commissioned Smith & Rhuland to build the schooner of his pre-*Bluenose* dreams, the *Gilbert B. Walters*, named for his sons, Gilbert and Bernard. If there was less to Angus Walters than international sportsmanship might have preferred, there was much more to him than outstanding schooner skills, as if those weren't enough. Given the many testimonials to his sailing and fishing abilities, and to his legendary foul temper, those aspects of his make-up are not in dispute. Much less is known about him as a community minded and committed citizen of Lunenburg, who contributed extensively to his bustling hometown.

Angus served on the Lunenburg Town Council for four years. He was a member of the Independent Order of Oddfellows (IOOF) and subsequently of the Masonic Order. It is an almost forgotten fact that when *Bluenose* first sailed out of Lunenburg in 1921, inscribed into her taffrail were the three horizontal links symbolizing the IOOF, a branch of the Masons. The links denote friendship, love, and truth—typical of the high-minded, unabashed values of the age.

Angus was a patron of the Order of the Eastern Star, a separate and unique order of Masons open to women. He was also an Orangeman, typical for a man of his times in an overwhelmingly Protestant town to whom fraternal connections clearly were important. Not too surprisingly, Angus became president of the Master Mariners' Association. Less predictably, given his business orientation and independent disposition, he was for two years president of the Lunenburg chapter of the upstart Fishermen's Federation of Nova Scotia, a union of fishermen formed in 1936 to seek increases in the price of haddock.

In 1937 the federation struck the big fish dealers, with fishermen tying up not just their own vessels but also the corporate fleets and the processing plants for three weeks before the government forced a compromise. Union boss was an unusual role for a banking-schooner skipper. But in the 1930s, bigger fish companies, some national, were redefining the industry, demonstrating that fishing captains often had more in common economically with their crews than with emerging giant companies.

Angus Walters was a leader, and if it was a local fishermen's union that needed leadership he was there to take the helm. As with his approach to everything, once in the union role Angus proved to be as "Bolshevist" as any coal-mining brother in Cape Breton. "I would like to

Ben Pine (left), owner and captain of Columbia *in 1923 and later master of the* Gertrude L. Thebaud, *could sometimes out-dress his friend and archrival Angus Walters, but he could rarely outsail him.*

ask some of [the wholesale dealers] who complain most loudly how much money their fathers left them—money that was made by the sweat of the men who sailed to the banks…." For Angus there clearly was no inconsistency between a job as a union leader and his various careers as a businessman. Ralph Getson, curator of education for the Lunenburg's Fisheries Museum of the Atlantic, observes that Angus's union role cost him friends, especially among Lunenburg's major business families, many of which had purchased shares in *Bluenose*. They reviled the union for all the usual reasons that business leaders do, and they regarded Angus's overt support as ingratitude and betrayal.

When *Bluenose* was retired as a banking schooner in 1939, Angus, too, went ashore for good. In another surprise, he soon turned away from the water altogether and towards one of the most totally land-based businesses of them all. He founded the Lunenburg Dairy. The dairy filled a gap in Lunenburg business and Angus ran it successfully for most of his remaining years. "You can whip our cream," his slogan ran. "But you can't beat our milk."

High on Gallows Hill overlooking Lunenburg is Hillcrest Cemetery. A modern granite stone marks Angus's resting place. One side acknowledges Angus's two wives, Maggie Tanner, the mother of his three sons, and Mildred Butler, "Dimples" to Angus, a former Halifax waitress who he married in 1939 after Maggie passed away. Mildred, thirty years Angus's junior, died in 1957 at forty-five; Angus in 1968, at eighty-seven.

The back of Angus's stone also serves as a marker for one of his brothers, Captain Perry L. Walters. Both sides of the stone display the Masonic emblem, the mason's compass and square enclosing the letter "G." The G is variously said to stand for God and for Geometry, comforts of equal utility onboard a banking schooner. Nowhere on the stone is there any mention of Angus Walters's mistress, the "black witch," *Bluenose*. It is the Lunenburg way, Ralph Getson said. "Perhaps he thought it might look too immodest."

CAPTAINS FROM CENTRAL CASTING

All vessels benefit from so-called "hard skippers," decisive if less malignant Ahabs and Blighs who know what to do in a crisis or at least know what to tell others to do. The *Bluenose II* mandate requires a captain with these core credentials, and many others. Angus Walters was decisive enough, but he would not have been well cast on *Bluenose II*, whose mission included domestic public relations and international tourist promotion, each requiring diplomacy and charm. Skippering *Bluenose II* has nothing to do with fishing or racing. It is not just about avoiding shoals either. A modern *Bluenose* master must comport himself with élan, not just on deck and at sea but also in the salons of Rosedale or Westmount, or even Young Avenue in Halifax. He, or she should that day ever come, must be equally at home in Yankee banquet halls of the northeastern US, where a tall ship's master can be as much of a celebrity as his vessel.

Captain Ernest Hartling, despite his misadventures, had many fine credentials when he took over *Bluenose II* in 1975. Indeed by one measure his first major trip, up the St. Lawrence to the Great Lakes and back, was a big success: one hundred thousand tourists visited *Bluenose*. Hartling, a worldly mariner with an easy grace, entertained them well. Unfortunately, he lacked other essential survival skills, political savvy first among them. Hartling possessed a near pathological reluctance to accept that *Bluenose II* had political as well as seagoing masters.

A few *Bluenose II* skippers simply would not or could not become public relations specialists, while at least two otherwise capable mariners knew little or nothing about sailing vessels and hoisted the schooner's sails as infrequently as possible. There were, of course, notable exceptions, well-rounded *Bluenose II* captains who seemed just right for the role.

If Angus Walters was a hard act to follow, even he might have found Captain Ellsworth Coggins, the very first captain of *Bluenose II,* a hard act to precede. Captain Coggins was the Oland's skipper, 1963 to 1970, and by most accounts, including his own, it was a shame he did not stay longer with the ship, at least to help get her through the rocky 1970s. Coggins came to *Bluenose II* fully-fledged, having taken *Bounty* from Lunenburg to Tahiti on her maiden voyage. That done, he continued as *Bounty*'s master for a European junket to promote *Mutiny on the Bounty.*

Captain Don Barr chats with passengers on a Bluenose II tour of Halifax Harbour. Barr sailed on Bluenose II *for nearly two decades and was her skipper for sixteen years. Gregarious and sociable, Barr was a well-regarded captain.*

Ellsworth Coggins was a sailing master of the old school. His ticket was in sail, not power. Only one other *Bluenose II* skipper, Wayne Walters, grandson of Angus, held such a ticket. Wayne was captain of the *Bluenose II* for a short stint in the 1990s. Today he is the province's director of operations for *Bluenose II*. Ellsworth Coggins took on *Bluenose* in 1963 as naturally as he had taken on *Bounty* when she was launched in 1960. He was regarded as a great sailing master. He was also a gregarious man who enjoyed the often thankless tedium of public mingling, representing not just the schooner's owners and Schooner lager, but often, unofficially, Nova Scotia and Canada. Under Captain Coggins, *Bluenose II* sailed through the 1960s respected and admired. Of course, as a privately owned vessel she was never subjected to the intense public scrutiny and media attention that government ownership would later attract.

With the tumultuous 1970s left safely astern, *Bluenose II* gradually picked up more favourable winds. It still took the new Progressive Conservative government, no doubt influenced by the affairs of the previous decade, nearly three years to renew the province's commitment to their sailing ambassador. At last they did, and the vessel was restored to respectable shape in 1983–84.

Equally significant, as of 1978 Don Barr had taken over as captain. His predecessor, Andrew Thomas, had been a good captain and a good Liberal who had come to the aid of his party. But he was neither a schooner man nor a tourist promoter. Barr was both; he'd already sailed on the schooner for a decade as second and then first mate, under various captains including Hartling and Thomas. For sixteen years, Captain Barr and his crew, with reasonable government support, kept *Bluenose II* respectable and generally in repair. Much of the work was tedious. Barr claims to have logged twenty thousand sea miles taking tourists around Halifax Harbour. But *Bluenose* never again experienced the ignominy of the "Gilbert and Sullivan" 1970s.

For Angus Walters, schooner command was more of a vocation than a choice; it seemed he could do no other. Don Barr had no such destiny. He was born in Saskatchewan, about as far away as you can get in Canada from the seafaring culture of the Atlantic. Increasingly during Barr's tenure as skipper, *Bluenose* business became Canadian consulate and corporate business, and the schooner became a much sought-after asset for Canadian trade missions. According to Barr, receptions on board *Bluenose* in Boston helped Bombardier sell railway cars to Amtrak. Only Angus Walters skippered a schooner called *Bluenose* for longer than Don Barr. Perhaps only Ellsworth Coggins and her current captain, Phil Watson, have skippered *Bluenose II* with comparable equanimity.

The current owners and handlers of the restored *Bluenose II* may wish to study both the Coggins and the Barr eras for tips on how best to run their impressive new sailing ambassador. As it happens, Captain Phil Watson has done just that. Ask anybody about Captain Watson and the answer will be the same—"a great guy." The quotable Ralph Getson of the Fisheries Museum pretty much summed up the general opinion: "I hold that man up with silk pins."

Captain Watson lives in a rambling yellow house in Mahone Bay with his wife, Krista, a physician and former *Bluenose* sailor; two kids, a large dog, a substantial *Bluenose* library and a lot of schooner paraphernalia. The latter includes two complete sets of the excellent L. B. Jenson measured drawings of *Bluenose II*. Phil Watson keeps one copy under his bed and another aboard *Bluenose* when the ship is touring. They are two of only one thousand sets in existence.

Captain Watson breaks many of the moulds of *Bluenose* masters. The schooner has been his only command, practically his only employer. He is

Captain Phil Watson of Mahone Bay was the last captain of the old Bluenose II *and will be the first captain of the newly restored vessel. He has been captain since 2001, having crewed on* Bluenose II *for fourteen years before that.*

transparently proud of *Bluenose II*, both as a complex sailing vessel to be professionally and smartly run, and as a cultural concept important to all Canadians.

"I have seen Albertans cry on the deck of *Bluenose II*, thrilled to actually see the boat when they had only seen it on the dime," Captain Watson says. "Kids love *Bluenose*, and they usually have no idea there ever was another *Bluenose*. My interest is getting as many kids as possible on board, from all across Canada." Phil Watson has his own vision of the real value of *Bluenose*. "She's a tangible part of history. What people don't know is how different life was back then, in the time of the banking schooners. How hard people had to work. How they had to make do. How dangerous it was. I think we have to do whatever we can to give people access to those days. That's what *Bluenose* does. It helps give them access."

Phil Watson's views should help Nova Scotians realize what *Bluenose* is, as well as what she is not. While there may be nothing wrong with the schooner promoting tourism and helping to pay her own costs, there are, or should be, some limits. "Selling *Bluenose II* for marketing purposes would be a no-brainer," says Bill Greenlaw, who heads the *Bluenose* project for the Department of Communities, Culture and Heritage. "But what are you willing to give up? *Bluenose* belongs to the people of Nova Scotia. Do you want Clearwater or a Royal Bank logo plastered across the mainsail?"

Greenlaw equates the value of *Bluenose* to the value of museums and historic monuments. "*Bluenose*," he says, "is not a commodity."

Captain Phil Watson would certainly agree.

Chapter XI

THE WAY OF A SCHOONER

There are three things which are too wonderful for me, yea, four which I know not:
The way of an eagle in the air; the way of a serpent upon a rock; the way of a ship in
the midst of the sea; and the way of a man with a maid.
-Proverbs 30: Verses 18,19

The most beautiful thing ever made by man for a purpose of utility.
-Captain Angus Walters, referring, of course, to Bluenose

Angus Walters would not have thought of himself as either an Old Testament prophet or a poet. He swore a lot, interpreted the rules creatively in a few of his famous races, and reamed out both crew and relatives whenever his famously cranky personality moved him to do so. But his juxtaposition of the notions of beauty and utility in his description of *Bluenose* comes as close as any poet has to capturing the enduring value of the schooner and the culture it inspired.

Historians and anthropologists hold to a common truth that a people must know and respect its past to comprehend its present and its future. The Nova Scotia fishery has multiple histories, but the prevailing folklore today is of the salt-fish banking enterprise, and of the impressive fleet of schooners that prosecuted it. In 1888 there were an estimated 193 salt bankers in Lunenburg alone. Combined with shipbuilding, and with the ancillary international trade generated by the huge

number of ships available, the salt-fish trade at its peak in the 1890s was the most vibrant enterprise in Nova Scotia's history.

If this time in our local history is remembered as a golden era of commerce and enterprise, it ought to be remembered too as an era unequalled for industrial death and destruction. The reality is that as the schooner age recedes to more than a century ago, it is best remembered now for having spawned the fastest and most handsome schooners afloat, and, in its dying days, for spawning *Bluenose*, the fastest of them all. The case for replicating, restoring, or otherwise saving *Bluenose* should reflect it all: the enterprise, the human sacrifices of crews and families, and the glory of the great schooner races. If she is to achieve Angus's "purpose of utility," the new *Bluenose* should sail in tribute to those memories, and to a time when Nova Scotia gave the world something special and enduring.

Among Nova Scotians, a thrifty and industrious lot, utility and beauty are much appreciated. *Bluenose* would be saluted anywhere as a handsome schooner. In Nova Scotia it may be the bonus factor of utility that adds an extra dimension. In practical Lunenburg, a vessel with credentials such as speed and beauty, and a utilitarian ability to earn a living for her owners, is not just admired. She is respected.

In Angus Walters's words, schooners are created for "the purpose of utility." They are also works of art. Even in rough weather they can display grace and competence. These startling photos show the original Bluenose (opposite), photographed by Wallace MacAskill, running before the wind sometime in the 1930s, and Bluenose II (left) absorbed by a heavy swell, photographed by Maurice Crosby, probably in the 1960s.

SCHOONER MYSTIQUE

Nova Scotians celebrate many aspects of their past. Unlike the great Gaels of Ireland, their wars have been few and not all that merry. But like those Gaels, their songs—plaintive laments of final farewells, of coal mining hardship, of privateering and schoonering—are often just as sad. There is pathos about schooners, of course, and especially about the bankers. The price in misery and lives lost paid by the men who sailed the bankers, and the hardships of lonely wives and widows, still haunts Lunenburg County. The stark pillars of the Fishermen's Memorial on Lunenburg's waterfront lists 128 vessels lost, 41 of them with all hands. The names of 692 sailors lost are inscribed on the memorial. The Fishermen's Memorial Cenotaph in Gloucester lists 5,377 fishermen who have died fishing out of that port since the 1600s. Of those, at least 1,200 were from Nova Scotia. But the response to this unspeakable carnage tends to be forgiving of the vessels themselves. In tragedy and death, the schooner generally was considered an innocent and even positive force.

Skippers such as Angus Walters always emerged from close calls crediting the virtues of the schooner. Seamanship and a twist of fate may have helped. But for every life a schooner took, the logic ran, she saved a hundred more. Schooners did not fail; only careless captains or rapacious owners did. Often when things went terribly wrong, the enemies were neither people nor schooners, but the vagaries of weather forecasting and the limited navigational technologies of a century ago.

Honoured for their speed and utility, schooners also are admired because they are works of art. Shipwrights and marine architects have more in common with sculptors than with tradespeople. It may be true that any shipwright can build a house, but not every carpenter can build a boat. Take a good look at a schooner and imagine trying to build one. While science clearly has a role—and much more so today than in the past—science alone will not get you there. On the hull of a schooner, little is square and less is plumb. The poet William Blake used the phrase "fearful symmetry" to describe a tiger. He might have been speaking of a schooner. Symmetry is essential, but somewhere in the building process, creative judgment and the artist's eye must rule. Sensibility and good taste must at times reject the blueprint and ignore both the level and the square.

It is no fluke that the most common piece of visual art on the walls of Nova Scotian homes—and of at least one McDonald's restaurant in Halifax—is neither a worthy Maud Lewis nor a stark Alex Colville. It is not a Group of

Seven, nor even a poster of Pittsburgh Penguins' Number 87. It invariably is a framed yellow-tinted reproduction of a photograph, instantly recognizable as one of the half-dozen best-known works of photographer W. R. MacAskill. The image is always of *Bluenose*, usually under full canvas, boiling to windward.

William J. Roué and Angus Walters were craftsmen and entrepreneurs. But they were artists, too. The ornery Angus, seen through the mists of time as a tough and practical man, may well have been a mystic when it came to sailing *Bluenose*. While Angus would have been the better sailor, he may have shared this compulsion with the mad poet Shelley. On July 8, 1822, Percy Bysshe Shelley drowned in Italy's Gulf of Spezia, sailing his tiny schooner *Don Juan* in a heavy gale. Clearly in more peril than he realized, Shelley refused an offer to be taken onboard a larger vessel, and he refused to shorten *Don Juan*'s sails.

Angus Walters used to say *Bluenose* "talked to him." Legend has it he sometimes would ask his crew to be quiet so he could hear her speak. In turn he would talk to her, cajole her during races, even bawl her out if she

Another classic photo of the original Bluenose *is called* Starboard Lookout, *taken by MacAskill in 1933. It hangs in hundreds of Canadian homes and businesses.*

underperformed: "Come on, you black witch!" (It has been rumored that Angus sometimes substituted "bitch" for "witch," depending on his mood.) Shelley, incidentally, said of his twenty-four-foot *Don Juan* that she "sailed like a witch." The very first book ever written about *Bluenose*, Andrew Merkel's 1948 *Schooner Bluenose*, described her as "a witch to windward." Richard Holmes, Shelley's masterful biographer, was even more poetic, referring to *Don Juan's* "swift temperamental elegance." Shelley's friend Edward Williams, who sailed and died with the poet on that fateful July day in 1822, had written of *Don Juan*, "she fetches whatever she looks at." Schooners inspire poets. They may even help create them.

INSIDE THE *BLUENOSE* BOW

Schooner mystique and artistry also surround the story about the prominent *Bluenose* bow and Angus Walters's role in it. Irresistible to every *Bluenose* writer, including

The symmetry of a schooner's bow rivals the "fearful symmetry" of a tiger, as described by poet William Blake. This pre-launch photo of Bluenose Now captures the imposing bow of the schooner, which some observers say will make her faster to windward, just like her famous forbears.

this one, the story goes that when the schooner was under construction Angus demanded that her bow be swept up an extra foot and a half, ostensibly to enhance comfort in the fo'c'sle sleeping quarters. It's possible. While Angus was not known to coddle his crew, he was known to respect them. Perhaps he wished to throw his crew a proverbial fish to preempt any grumbling about his own minor shipboard luxuries, such as the brass bed he ordered for his cabin.

Designer William J. Roué did not draw the *Bluenose* bow as it was built. By his own admission he did not oppose it either; not in the face of the short and fierce skipper with the tall personality, who also happened to be one of the schooner's major shareholders. It is equally possible, of course, that Angus saw something even Bill Roué did not. There is little doubt that the distinct upward lunge of the *Bluenose* bow helped her shed water as she drove to windward. Apart from issues of style and grace, there are serious sailing buffs who claim it was precisely this feature that gave *Bluenose* her unrivalled velocity to weather for a schooner of her size and type.

Claude Darrach, the only crewmember of the original *Bluenose* to have written extensively about her, made this observation, in a lovely, and poetic, 1985 memoir called *Race to Fame*:

Her design was slightly different to the previous conventional schooners.… Some schooners, carrying all sail under strong wind force, will bury and drag water. Too much green water will tumble on deck…Bluenose tended to heave out, but shipped no water on deck and maintained a stable equilibrium at all times. When she was under full sail and the gusts of wind had a force of 35 m.p.h. coming in from forward of the beam, with sheets trimmed she would show a high windward side, while the lee still maintained a stable center of buoyancy, enabling her to cope with and benefit from the wind force…I believe this explains what the experienced shipwrights were talking about when they referred to her as "different."

Fortunately, Angus himself is on the record regarding the matter of the *Bluenose* bow. Unfortunately, as is often the case with Angus, his comments invite interpretation. Both the Fisheries Museum of the Atlantic and the archives of the Canadian Broadcasting Corporation have video copies of a rare television interview with Angus conducted in the mid-1960s by the CBC broadcasting giant, J. Frank Willis. Willis also interviewed William Roué. He asked them both about the *Bluenose* bow. Roué's reply was conventional: "Angus wanted more room in the fo'c'sle," he said resignedly. Angus's comment was enigmatic. "It didn't slow her down. It had no effect...." Then, after a pause… "It made her a drier boat. And you don't want water on deck racing, if you can help it." Whether or not it made her faster, the turn of the *Bluenose* bow gave the schooner something else: a slight demeanor of either arrogance or vague contempt; attitudes not unheard of in her captain.

ONE QUESTION, MANY ANSWERS

At the Fisheries Museum of the Atlantic in Lunenburg, the excellent *Bluenose* exhibit advances three theories to explain *Bluenose* success as a racing schooner.

1. Last minute changes in the hull—the Angus touch
2. Frost "setting" her timbers while she was under construction
3. Her captain and crew

Never far from the debate, and not necessarily under oath, Angus himself helped foster the "frost" theory of what made the schooner that was built the schooner she became. "It was the way her spars was set. If the rest of her is good, a vessel's spars will pretty well tell what she'll do. Somehow, the *Bluenose's* spars was set mathematically perfect, in a way that no man could do. I think that was it."

Over time the prevailing and most tenable theory about *Bluenose* racing success has been rooted in the fact that size matters. Marq de Villiers's well-researched book *Witch in the Wind* purports to be "the true story of the legendary *Bluenose*." No small ambition. To that end de Villiers is among the few writers to emphasize a fundamental fact about *Bluenose*: she was bigger than many of the vessels she raced against. *Elsie*, the 1921 US competitor skippered by Nova Scotian Marty Welch, was only 106 feet overall. *Bluenose* was 143 feet. It is a well-known aspect of sailing dynamics that bigger and longer in a sailing vessel usually mean faster.

"Yes, but," you can hear a chorus cry.

Yes, but! Just a goddamned minute now.... *Columbia* was 141 feet overall. Could 3 feet make a difference?

Yes, but the *Gertrude L. Thebaud* was only 99 feet on the water line to *Bluenose's* 112, and she whipped *Bluenose* pretty smartly in the 1930 Lipton Cup race.

Yes, but the Fishermen's Trophy was not at stake in 1930, and in 1931 and again in 1938, when it was, *Bluenose* took care of *Thebaud*....

Then comes the high card of all the "yes, buts": the Nova Scotian schooner *Haligonian* was almost a replica of *Bluenose*; a shade bigger, in fact; designed by Bill Roué no less, and built primarily to put *Bluenose* in her place. And look what happened: *Bluenose* cleaned her clock.

There is a formula to determine the theoretical "maximum" speed of a sailing vessel: "One and one-third times the square root of the water-line length in feet." L. B. Jenson, in his notes for his *Bluenose II* drawings in *Saga of the Great Fishing Schooners,* acknowledges this formula, but adds a caveat: "In fact, however, it has been proven that under certain conditions of the sea combined with very high winds, *Bluenose II* has exceeded her maximum theoretical speed."

In earlier drafts of his design for *Bluenose,* (the one finally selected was Number 17), Roué had fixed *Bluenose*'s waterline at 120 feet, presumably to enhance both her stability and speed. That design was rejected. The *Herald*'s Deed of Gift for the Fishermen's Trophy stipulated a maximum length for the schooners of 145 feet, and at that length her waterline would have been excessive. Speculation at the time was that publisher William Dennis was aware of the fast Gloucester schooner *Elizabeth Howard*, 148 feet, eight inches long, and, since Dennis was writing the rules, he took the opportunity to write her out of contention.

Yes but, Dennis drew up the Deed of Gift before Roué was ever asked to design *Bluenose*. Roué almost certainly would have been happy to have made her 155 feet if necessary. Indeed, the overall length under the deed was later amended to 155 feet, giving rise to conjecture that should a new Canadian schooner be needed she would be at maximum length. Such a schooner, it was rumoured, would then be bigger than any vessel that could be safely launched on the shallow Essex River where most American contenders were built.

Captain Don Barr, skipper of *Bluenose II* for sixteen years, has an experienced sailor's response to predictable questions about *Bluenose*'s speed. "It was waterline length. *Bluenose* never raced against boats with her waterline length." William J. Roué said that he "designed her to carry sail," deliberately keeping her centre of gravity low, a stability feature in all sailing vessels. Once asked the same "secret of success" question at a *Bluenose* seminar, writer Silver Donald Cameron had a different but equally confident answer: "Luck and Angus Walters."

Chapter XII

GRANDFATHER'S *BLUENOSE*

I still have Grandfather's axe. Father replaced the helve and I replaced the blade. The axe is better than ever.

-Newfoundland folk saying

If I were to go blind, I'd want people to take me sailing.

-Harry Bruce, "Each Moment As It Flies"

Despite his efforts to demythologize *Bluenose*, even Marq de Villiers could not resist attributing anthropomorphic and magical powers to the schooner. He refers to her "peculiar genius" when sailing to windward in the race against *Elsie*. His book, *Witch in the Wind*, presents the schooner as demonic and bewitched, a bit like Shelley's *Don Juan*.

Writing about the *Bluenose* schooners of yesterday, nearly every author has been smitten by their seductive ways. An introduction to the 1955 edition of G. J. Gillespie's *Bluenose Skipper* was penned by the former Nova Scotia premier and senator, Harold Connolly. His words were a spirited blend of unrestrained ardor for *Bluenose*, and editorial rant.

OPPOSITE
Bluenose *and* Columbia *crewmembers, photographed in Halifax in 1923. Angus Walters is front row, centre. If the new* Bluenose *is not sailed hard like the original, one reason, according to* Bluenose II *Captain Phil Watson, is that Walters's racing crew was made up of twenty or more veteran fishermen and sailors, many of them experienced captains of other schooners who would sign on with Angus for the big races.*

She was a queen, and like all queens, she had a date with destiny. But here was a royal lady who might have been preserved for all time in all her royal trimmings...

Representing, as she did, a link with the days that are no more, she might have told, mutely it is true, but effectively nonetheless, of that era when Nova Scotia was a power upon the oceans of the world. We owed that much to Bluenose...

When, however, the mantle of time fell around her shoulders, we did not so much as honour her with an old-age pension. What in the world were we thinking about?

What were they thinking about? Angus Walters had posed a similar question himself in a letter to the *Chronicle Herald* in 1963.

I did not want to sell her, but circumstances compelled me to do so and I feel to the shame of the province and the Town of Lunenburg, and citizens who were in a position to have set up the Bluenose as a permanent memorial of a fast-dying way of fishing, that she was allowed to go south to flounder and rest on a bed of rocks.

THE TRUE *BLUENOSE* LEGACY

Amid the sentimentality of former politicians and the understandable resentment of an aging captain, there are useful messages from the past that we can channel today.

It should be remembered first that the overall outcome of the Fishermen's Trophy races, regardless of schooner size, was no small achievement for *Bluenose*. Most of her victories were decisive; many demonstrated superior tactical skills by her captain and crew, and most of them showed convincingly that her ability to foot to windward was more than just a matter of a few feet of waterline, or a few extra tons of weight.

To merely qualify for each international race, *Bluenose* usually had to knock out several Nova Scotia schooners built in her mould. To earn the right to compete for Canada in 1921, for instance, *Bluenose* had to outpace seven worthy domestic schooners, including the ever-dangerous *Delawana* and, even more threatening, *Canadia*, newly built in Shelburne especially to strike fear into the hearts of Lunenburgers. *Canadia*, at 138 feet—about the same size as *Columbia*—was designed and built by seventy-one-year-old Amos Pentz, and skippered by Joe Conrad of LaHave, also in his seventies at the time—gentlemen who knew their schooners.

In the first of two races *Canadia* competed well, finishing second four minutes behind *Bluenose*. In race two, *Bluenose* left all competitors far behind, characteristically opening up a wide gap on the windward leg. The *Bluenose* edge was obvious, as it would be against *Elsie* for the trophy that year, and as it would remain be for years to come.

A MacAskill photo of the 1921 race shows *Elsie's* bow plunging deep into the water, unable to comfortably carry the increasing spread of canvas her combative captain, Marty Welch, piled on. The thrashing continued until *Elsie* lost her foretopmast, leaving her no hope of winning. The differences between *Bluenose* and *Elsie* illustrated the importance of size. Less directly it commented on the *Bluenose* bow. "What *Elsie* needed," writer Keith McLaren concluded, "was more hull in the water, not more sail aloft."

Perhaps Nova Scotia shipwrights really did build better schooners; or, an even more chauvinistic thought, perhaps the rugged Nova Scotia coast produced more competent skippers, just as it produced at least one— Angus Walters—more wily than all the others. This contention has some weight. Two of the Gloucester skippers who threatened *Bluenose* most, Marty Welch and Clayt Morrissey, were Nova Scotians. *Columbia's* and *Thebaud's* estimable master, meanwhile, was the transplanted Newfoundlander, Ben Pine.

In a moment of folly during a windy 1921 race, Captain Marty Welch of Elsie *tries to match canvas with Angus, "the bugger to carry sail." The much smaller* Elsie's *foretopmast comes crashing down. Ahead in the race, and with the kind of sporting gesture for which he was not exactly famous, Angus dropped his "ballooner" sail to roughly match* Elsie's *crippled rig.*

Beyond her victories in races and her fishing "utility" and success, the original *Bluenose* was an impressive piece of design and construction. Her two successors were and are no different. People who have had the privilege of seeing Bluenose Now up close during construction won't forget the experience. Few people realize just how much of a schooner is below the waterline. Viewed out of the water, her size, symmetry and craftsmanship are startling.

Schooner owners and masters in the 1920s tended to be hardworking and tough. But like Gloucester's Ben Pine, a blown-away Newfoundlander, they also were gentlemen of standing and often of means. Ashore they dressed sharply, and it was not uncommon for them to don jackets and ties on civil days aboard their schooners.

When Lathan B. Jenson produced his meticulous scaled drawings of *Bluenose II* in the mid-1970s, he used a simple device to illustrate the schooner's size. He drew tiny, scaled figures of six-foot tall men, usually carrying an adze or an axe, next to the schooner to illustrate her height relative to a moderately tall human. A six-foot-tall man standing at the after end of the keel, looking straight up to the stern of the vessel where the rudder is hung, would have fifteen feet of clearance above his head. If he were standing at the bow looking straight up at the bowsprit, there would be at least twenty feet.

FIRST-HAND EXPERIENCE

The experience of seeing the schooner out of the water could be a greater thrill for an admirer who takes an extra moment to imagine the original *Bluenose* in her element, perhaps during that wild April gale of 1926.

Angus is lashed to the wheel. The entire 285 tons of schooner, trapped close to a lee shore, is blown down nearly to her beam-ends and she is bucking like a massive bronco. It was a miracle *Bluenose* survived that storm; many schooners didn't. Merely imagining such a scene would be adventure enough for most people. Actually being there was another matter.

The late Clem Hiltz was one of the longest surviving members of the original *Bluenose* crews. He was ninety-two in 2003 when he was interviewed by Adrian Humphreys, a reporter for the National Post. In Hiltz's account of that fearful night, reality and *Bluenose* mythology seem to merge.

Angus Walters stood lashed to that wheel for eight long hours. You think the adult population can't pray? I assure you they can pray and they learned me how to that night. We made a decision that when she gets stuck, we'd take each other by the hand and jump overboard together. We didn't

want to be buried in the sand. We wanted to die
in the sea. But it never happened. Captain Walters
took us across the bar and saved our lives.

According to Hiltz, 130 men lost their lives that night on other ships. "I lost a lot of relations, cousins and uncles—but nobody was lost on *Bluenose*."

Bluenose made it back to Lunenburg missing two anchors, three hundred fathoms of cable, and some fishing gear. Clem Hiltz, on his first trip to the Banks at the age of 14, undoubtedly lost his childhood. The official death toll of the night was 138. Angus Walters described the storm as the "worst in the history of fishermen." The next image for a Lunenburg tourist might well be that granite waterfront monument honouring the hundreds of men who died for food and family on vessels very much like *Bluenose*.

REPLICAS AND REBUILDS

Will Bluenose Now sail like Angus's *Bluenose*, or even like *Bluenose II* in her own salad days? If she does, it will not be because she is exactly like her forbears. It will be because she will be an outstanding vessel in her own right, skippered by some modern bugger to carry sail.

The "replica" of *Bounty* was 180 feet long, built 30 percent bigger than the original in order to accommodate cameras and the general clutter and hubbub of a movie set. The new reproduction of *Columbia* is made of steel. Like these vessels, Bluenose Now ultimately is a concept and not a true copy. However, as a wooden schooner built in Lunenburg, maintaining the external dimensions of both previous *Bluenoses*, she is a more direct descendant, closer to her forebears, than either *Bounty* or *Columbia*. If her role is to evoke the past, she will be successful.

As for the shibboleths about restorations and rebuilds, it is at least entertaining to pose an existential question: Is it more important to have grandfather's axe or an axe just like grandfather's, only better? The question may be best left to the realms of Zen and philosophy. Nova Scotians and Canadians cannot have the original *Bluenose* back. Her broken hull was last seen on a reef off Haiti in 1946. Nor will the "original" *Bluenose II* ever sail again, except in the highly notional form of the remnants and parts that were salvaged, repaired and installed on Bluenose Now.

The controversy that swirled briefly around the question of restoration was a storm in a teapot. True, some took it more seriously than others. Not long after the *Bluenose* restoration announcement in 2009, an angry blogger for the Halifax Shipping News invoked the example of Japanese pagodas dating back to 706 AD

to demonstrate how absurd, in his view, the *Bluenose* restoration idea really was. "While no single piece [of the pagodas] actually dates back to 706," the blogger revealed, "each piece shares a lineage and existed with the other pieces at a moment in time. The temple is not torn down periodically and replaced every 40 years when the rot shows up. The bad pieces are refreshed." How many angels can dance on the masthead of a schooner? At least today's *Bluenose* actually carries a few pieces dating back to 1963 or before. And there certainly is sufficient *Bluenose II* oxygen in the new boat to meet Tom Gallant's modest standard.

Speaking for the province in December 2012, Michael Noonan of Communications Nova Scotia noted that *Bluenose II* was never an exact replica of the original schooner *Bluenose*, but "more of a representation," and that "this continues to be the case with this restoration." Representation is not a bad concept. It nicely dodges the question of what exactly tomorrow's *Bluenose* must be, leaving the decision to all of us. We can make of her whatever we wish.

Ultimately, *Bluenose* is a metaphor and a touchstone. She is a metaphor for a people's quest and ambition, for their daring and their toughness, and frequently for their folly, at a unique moment in their history. She is also a touchstone for all who hold the conviction that

to live in ignorance of the past is to live in ignorance of the present, and all who understand how physical representations of the past can help us understand and bring us closer to it.

Today's *Bluenose* preserves and carries forward the spirit the original. She pays tribute to a high-mettle time when the Nova Scotia schooner meant victory and international success, especially against the lordly Americans. One of the most impressive Gloucester schooner writers was Joseph E. Garland. In *Down to the Sea: The Fishing Schooners of Gloucester*, Garland wrote with empathy about the 1920 *Esperanto* versus *Delawana* race and what the loss meant to Canada. He set the table for the two decades of rancour that followed.

Thus good-naturedly enough commenced the nineteen-year racing rivalry between Gloucester and Lunenburg, the United States and Canada.

Except that for a couple of centuries the Canadians had endured the larceny of their mackerel and their herring at the hands of the invading Americans, and of their best fishermen enticed by the US dollar to Gloucester—and now, from under their blue noses, the grand larceny of what one and all had been so sure was to be their very own for keeps, a Canada's Cup!

If it took an American writer to evoke the sense of Canadian grievance and the magnitude of the injury that helped create *Bluenose*, other prominent Yankees preferred to stoke the fires of acrimony. Celebrating *Esperanto*'s 1920 Fishermen's Cup win, Calvin Coolidge, then governor of Massachusetts and subsequently the thirtieth president of the United States, found himself in manifest destiny mode. "A triumph of Americanism," he declared. "Our wonderful victory shows to all the world what Massachusetts stands for and what America is bound to accomplish."

Looking towards tomorrow, it may take a quiet and committed Canadian to bring the *Bluenose* goods forward, to lead the new schooner in a manner that understands and amplifies her meaning.

Phil Watson is a reflective man who has commanded *Bluenose II* since 2001. He took over as master following fourteen years before her mast, working his way up from deckhand to third, second and first mate; finally to skipper. On the question of restorations, rebuilds and construction materials, Captain Watson is sanguine: "What matters is that she is a wooden schooner on the outside. If they want to put steel knees or ribs in to make her strong and last longer, that's fine."

As the *Bluenose* centenary approaches, Nova Scotians and all Canadians might reflect on the stark fact that *Bluenose* is not about what *might* have been. She is about what was. *Bluenose* messages from the distant past can be deciphered this way: *Bluenose* represents an era of skill and enterprise and art, and of commercial fishing success. Nova Scotians might wish to follow her example and strive for the ethos and the values that enabled that success. *Bluenose* also represents a darker time when the lives of workers were devalued currency and when most fishermen and their families sacrificed far too much for far too little. So the schooner should remind us of that fact too, the opposite side of the dime. Only when we use our icons smartly, when we refuse to let them trick us into a one-dimensional view of the past, do we realize their value. This is why *Bluenose* lives. That is how she can have a "purpose of utility", in an age in search of its own bearings and touchstones.

For at least the next half-century Canadians and schooner junkies everywhere will continue to ogle the great schooner, oohing and aahing as they've done since 1920. Younger Canadians will, for the first time, fall in love with the ship on the dime. In turn, their own grandchildren will hear stories about the *Bluenose* until the end of the twenty-first century.

The schooner with the glorious past has a shot at a glorious future.

NOTE ON SOURCES

Today's *Bluenose* may be virtually a new schooner, but she is hardly a new subject for writers. She has been written about and discussed incessantly for almost a century.

At least fifteen books have "Bluenose" in their titles and scores and perhaps hundreds of others have references, sections, or chapters on the schooner. The Internet is a cornucopia of information—albeit highly repetitive and frequently distracting. It is a great source for tips and comparisons, though there are few original sources online.

This book recounts the restoration of *Bluenose II*, or "Bluenose Now." However, the newly restored schooner has little meaning and no purpose without the context of *Bluenose* history and mythology, and so I have included as much of both as possible.

I owe a huge debt to writers, broadcasters, and filmmakers who have created their own books, documents, and programs about the schooner. I appreciate and respect their efforts. In sections where I have relied directly on their accounts or interpretations, I have been careful to acknowledge their works. In cases where they have made points more effectively than I could, I have quoted short excerpts intact.

The bibliography lists only works that I have used in some direct way, either by quotation, for clarification of dates and names or other details, or for inspiration. Many more works appeared on my radar and vanished without impact.

Three books were disproportionately informative and impressive, and each is cited several times in the text. Keith McLaren's *A Race for Real Sailors* is the bible of the International Fishermen's Cup races that made the original *Bluenose* famous. Published in 2006, it is nicely illustrated with the best photos available, including some taken by McLaren himself as a onetime *Bluenose II* crewmember.

In 1984 Silver Donald Cameron wrote a spirited book called *Schooner: Bluenose and Bluenose II,* after a voyage on *Bluenose II* from Lunenburg to Atlantic

City. The book was republished in 1992 under the title *Once Upon a Schooner*. This later version includes an amusing epilogue that anticipates the eventual birth of a "Bluenose III," forecasting the debate over how to build and pay for her. I am indebted to Cameron's writing, and to Captain Don Barr, who sat still for two long interviews, for details of *Bluenose II*'s 1970s adventures and misadventures.

Only one author has attempted to write a definitive book about *Bluenose*. Marq de Villiers' *Witch in the Wind* is meticulous and thorough. It sails close to its worthy goal, and is both a good read and a reliable reference work. Today, of course, with the new *Bluenose II* schooner rigged and ready, a definitive account of the schooner is farther away than ever.

There are numerous older and more modest books worth noting; books that too often have been dismissed as either solicitous or amateur. In my view their value is ever increasing, mainly because they were closer to original sources, such as Angus Walters himself, and to many of his *Bluenose* crewmembers. Among those smaller treasures are Andrew Merkel's *Schooner Bluenose* (1948); G. J. Gillespie's *Bluenose Skipper* (1955); Claude Darrach's *Race to Fame: The Inside Story of the Bluenose* (1985); and *Bluenose: Queen of the Grand Banks*, by Feenie and Zeke Ziner.

I am grateful to those and many other writers and researchers who have gone before, and I am pleased to make my own contribution to the evolving and always intriguing story of the people's schooner.

BIBLIOGRAPHY

Andersen, Raoul. *Voyage to the Grand Banks: The Saga of Captain Arch Thornhill*. St. John's: Creative Publishing, 1998.

Backman, Brian, and Phil Backman. *Bluenose*. Toronto: McClelland and Stewart, 1965.

Bartlett, Bob. *Sails over Ice: Northern Adventures aboard the SS Morrissey*. St. John's: Flanker, 2008.

Bluenose II Rebirth of the Legend. Lunenburg: Lunenburg Shipyard Alliance, 2012.

Bruce, Harry. *Each Moment as It Flies: Writings*. Toronto: Methuen, 1984.

Cameron, Silver Donald. *Once Upon A Schooner: An Offshore Voyage in Bluenose II*. Halifax: Formac, 1992.

Cameron, Silver Donald. *Schooner: Bluenose and Bluenose II*. Toronto: Seal, 1984.

Chapelle, Howard Irving. *The History of American Sailing Ships*. New York: W. W. Norton, 1935.

Choyce, Lesley. *Nova Scotia: Shaped by the Sea–A Living History*. Lawrencetown, NS: Pottersfield, 2007.

Coles, K. Adlard. *Heavy Weather Sailing*. London: Adlard Coles, 1967.

Crew, Bob. *Sea Poems: A Seafarer Anthology*. Rendlesham, Suffolk, England: Seafarer, 2005.

Daniels, Jane. *The Illustrated Dictionary of Sailing*. New York: Friedman Group, 1989.

Darrach, Claude K. *Race to Fame: The Inside Story of the Bluenose*. Hantsport, NS: Lancelot, 1985.

DeVilliers, Marq. *Witch in the Wind: The True Story of the Legendary Bluenose*. Toronto: Thomas Allen, 2007.

Dyson, John, and Peter Christopher. *Spirit of Sail: On Board the World's Great Sailing Ships*. Toronto: Key Porter, 1987.

Fergusson, Charles Bruce. *Joseph Howe of Nova Scotia*. Windsor, NS: Lancelot, 1973.

Finlay-de Monchy, Marike, and Karin Cope. *Casting a Legend: The Story of the Lunenburg Foundry*. Halifax: Nimbus, 2002.

Garland, Joseph E. *Bear of the Sea: Giant Jim Patillo and the Roaring Years of the Gloucester-Nova Scotia Fishery*. Halifax: Nimbus, 2001.

Garland, Joseph E. *Down to the Sea: The Fishing Schooners of Gloucester*. Boston: D. R. Godine, 1983.

Getson, Heather-Anne. *Bluenose: The Ocean Knows Her Name*. Halifax: Nimbus, 2006.

Gillespie, Gerald Joseph. *Bluenose Skipper: the Story of the Bluenose and Her Skipper*. Fredericton: Brunswick Press, 1964.

Graham, Monica. *Bluenose*. Halifax: Nimbus, 2010.

Hartling, Ernest K., and Jo Kranz. *Bluenose Master: The Memoirs of Captain Ernest K. Hartling*. Willowdale, ON: Hounslow, 1989.

Henderson, Richard. *Understanding Rigs and Rigging*. Camden, ME: International Marine Publishing, 1991.

Hollingsworth, Alan. *The Way of a Yacht: An Introduction to the Comparative Anatomy of Offshore Sailing Craft*. New York: Norton, 1974.

Holmes, Richard. *Shelley: The Pursuit*. London: Quartet, 1976.

Holy Bible. N.P.: Ottenheimer, 1973.

Jenson, Lathan B. *Bluenose II: Saga of the Great Fishing Schooners*. Halifax: Nimbus, 1994.

Junger, Sebastian. *The Perfect Storm: A True Story of Men Against the Sea*. New York: Norton, 1997.

Kurlansky, Mark. *Cod: A Biography of the Fish That Changed the World*. Toronto: Alfred Knopf Canada, 1997.

Langille, Jacqueline. *Captain Angus Walters*. Tantallon, NS: Four East Publications, 1990.

Lever, Darcy. *The Young Sea Officer's Sheet Anchor: Or A Key to the Leading of Rigging and to Practical Seamanship*. Ottawa: Algrove Limited, 2000.

March, William. *Red Line: The Chronicle-Herald and the Mail-Star, 1875–1954*. Halifax: Chebucto Agencies, 1986.

McLaren, Keith. *Bluenose & Bluenose II*. Willodale: Hounslow, 1981.

———. *A Race for Real Sailors: The Bluenose and the International Fishermen's Cup, 1920–1938*. Vancouver: Douglas & McIntyre, 2006.

Merkel, Andrew Doane, and Wallace R. MacAskill. *Schooner Bluenose*. Toronto: Ryerson, 1948.

Parker, John P. *Sails of the Maritimes*. Aylesbury: Hazell Watson & Viney, 1969.

Parker, Mike. *Historic Lunenburg: The Days of Sail*. Halifax: Nimbus, 1999.

Payzant, Joan M. *Halifax: Cornerstone of Canada*. Halifax: Windsor Publications, 1985.

Plaskett, Bill. *Understanding Lunenburg's Architecture*. Lunenburg: Lunenburg Heritage Society, 1989.

Pullen, H. F. *Atlantic Schooners*. Fredericton: Brunswick, 1967.

Roberts, Harry D., and Michael O. Nowlan. *Sailing Ships of Newfoundland: The Newfoundland Fish Boxes*. St. John's: Breakwater, 1986.

Robinson, Bill. *The Great American Yacht Designers*. New York: Knopf, 1974.

Roue, Joan. *A Spirit Deep Within: Naval Architect W. J. Roué and the Bluenose Story*. Hantsport, NS: Lancelot, 1995.

Smyth, W. H. *The Sailor's Word-Book: An Alphabetical Digest of Nautical Terms*. Almonte, ON: Algrove Limited, 2004.

Spicer, Stanley T. *The Age of Sail: Master Shipbuilders of the Maritimes*. Halifax: Formac, 2001.

Spicer, Stanley T. *Masters of Sail: the Era of Square-rigged Vessels in the Maritime Provinces*. Toronto: Ryerson, 1968.

Stapleton, Berni, Chris Brookes, and Jamie Lewis. *They Let Down Baskets*. St. John's: Killick Press, 1998.

Taylor, M. Brook. *A Camera on the Banks: Frederik William Wallace and the Fishermen of Nova Scotia*. Fredericton: Goose Lane, 2006.

Thomas, Gordon W. *Fast & Able: Life Stories of Great Gloucester Fishing Vessels*. Ed. Paul B. Kenyon. Gloucester, MA: Gloucester 350th Anniversary Celebration, Inc. 1973.

Thornton, Tim. *The Offshore Yacht*. London: Adlard Coles, 1984.

Villiers, Alan John. *Men, Ships, and the Sea*. Washington, DC: National Geographic Society, 1962.

Winchester, Simon. *Atlantic*. New York: HarperCollins, 2010.

Ziner, Feenie, and Zeke Ziner. *Bluenose: Queen of the Grand Banks*. Philadelphia: Chilton Book, 1970.

IMAGE CREDITS

MARK DOUCETTE
All *Bluenose II* restoration photos

NOVA SCOTIA ARCHIVES
Aerial View, Bluenose II *under sail* 19
Bluenose II *being refitted at Smith & Rhuland, Lunenburg,*
    NS 24
Launch of Bluenose II 16
Captain and visitors on board Bluenose II 83

PHOTOGRAPHED BY W. R. MACASKILL
Bluenose, *Halifax Harbour, 1931* XIV
Columbia *1923* 10
Haligonian *(Sail No. 2)* 12
Bluenose *in a Seaway* 88
Starboard Lookout 91
Bluenose *Crew* 96
Grand Bank Fishing Schooner Elsie *losing topmast* 99

COURTESY OF MAURICE CROSBY
Bluenose II, *The Legend Continues* (main cover) 22, 89

PHOTOGRAPHS BY LESLIE JONES,
    COURTESY OF BOSTON PUBLIC LIBRARY
Ben Pine and Angus Walters, Gloucester, 1930 81
Pennants Flying off Fishing Schooner, 1930 47
Ben Pine, 1923 100
Bluenose *Racing* Henry Ford 8

MARITIME MUSEUM OF THE ATLANTIC
FREDERICK WILLIAM WALLACE COLLECTION
Capt. Walters at the wheel 76
Capt. Walters, close up, standing with long coat on 78

RON CROCKER

Ron is a journalist and a retired television producer and executive. He worked with the Canadian Broadcasting Corporation for more than thirty years. Ron grew up in Heart's Delight, NL, and graduated from Memorial University of Newfoundland and Osgoode Hall Law School in Toronto. He lives in Glen Haven, NS, with Sheila Fitzpatrick and their son Robin. When not reading or writing about boats, Ron sails his Contessa 32, *Fifth of July*, out of French Village Harbour.

MARK DOUCETTE

Mark Doucette is a professional photographer and a retired teacher. He taught in the Dartmouth and Halifax school systems for thirty-two years, and gave numerous workshops in photography along the way. Mark grew up in Bedford, Nova Scotia, and graduated from St. Mary's University with degrees in Commerce and Education, and Dalhousie University with an M.A. He lives in St. Margaret's Bay, Nova Scotia, with his wife, Suzanne. When not shooting on the *Bluenose II* or some other photo assignment, Mark can be found sailing or kayaking or cycling in and around the St. Margaret's Bay area. He is most proud of the fact that he is father to John, Sarah, and Lee.

Mark Doucette Photographic is the official photographer of the *Bluenose II* restoration. Visit mdphoto.ca